Thinking of...

The Internet of Things from the Director's Perspective?

Ask the Smart Questions

By David Goad & Stephen Parker

Smart Questions™ Philosophy

Smart Questions is built on 3 key pillars, which set it apart from other publishers:

1. *Smart people want Smart Questions not Dumb Answers*
2. *Domain experts are often excluded from authorship, so we are making writing a book simple and painless*
3. *The community has a great deal to contribute to enhance the content*

www.smart-questions.com

Foreword

Today's fiction is tomorrow's reality and the Internet of Things will be a key part of shaping this future. The effect of IoT will be unprecedented, changing every aspect of our business and private lives. It may be more appropriate to refer to IoT as the Impact of Things.

IoT holds the promise to dramatically increase industrial productivity and improve customer service. There is also the potential for enormously positive social impacts through enhanced food security, improvements to the environment and a radically different approach to healthcare.

However, such major changes will also create challenges and as company directors and executives it is essential that we consider how this new reality will shape our business landscape before we jump into solving mode.

Thinking of…The Internet of Things from the Director's Perspective? Ask the Smart Questions" is timely. It is published as IoT adoption reaches an inflection point where every major company needs to consider what IoT means to its future success. Although formulating an IoT strategy will be an ongoing process, now is the time to begin.

Stephen and David have skillfully provided an overview and context for IoT innovation within the greater digital disruption that is undoubtedly the hallmark of the 21st century. They successfully break down the different aspects and simplify the strategic view. They make it easier for us all to ask the smart questions and shape the problems which are fundamental to developing the best solutions.

This strategic thinking will be essential to help manage investment decisions, whether external capital or internal budgeting, as well as the mode of engagement with external parties such as consultants and technology providers. Everything IoT is proud to be involved with this ground-breaking corporate IoT guide, ensuring that leaders have the framework and insight they needed to capitalize on the opportunities made available by the IoT revolution.

These are exciting times and the opportunities for those who can embrace change whilst managing the risks will be enormous. I wish you all the success in harnessing the power of IoT for the future of your business and the world we share.

Eitan Bienstock, Director and Founder,
Everything IoT, https://www.everythingiot.com.au/

Authors

Stephen Parker (GAICD, MACS Snr CP)

A translator between Directors, CxO's and IT Pros, connecting Digital Transformation to Business Transformation.

With over 30 years of business transformation experience, Stephen provides creative and challenging thinking that aligns essential business needs with innovative technology.

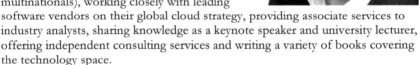

He has gained experience in executive leadership roles (from startups to multinationals), working closely with leading software vendors on their global cloud strategy, providing associate services to industry analysts, sharing knowledge as a keynote speaker and university lecturer, offering independent consulting services and writing a variety of books covering the technology space.

(www.linkedin.com/in/sjkparker)

David Goad (P.Eng. MBA PMP CPIM)

David has over 30 years of industry experience having held senior leaderships roles with recognized IT brands such as KPMG Consulting, Microsoft and Hitachi Solutions. A consummate entrepreneur David has created his own successful IT start-up, built it up to being a global award-winning business and then sold it off. Currently a Post-Graduate Fellow at Sydney University, David teaches at both Sydney University and the University of New South Wales in the areas of Innovation, Business Applications, Digital Business Management and Accounting Information Systems. His research areas are the Internet of Things, Business Models and Innovation. A published author he has presented his work on IoT Architecture at the American Conference on Information Systems. He is a member of the IoT Association of Australia and provides consulting advice to entrepreneurs starting new businesses and to enterprises developing their IoT strategy.

(www.linkedin.com/in/dgoad/)

Reviews

This book asks all the right questions about every stage of the IoT process, especially questions pertaining to how your implementation will affect the Customer Experience. The book allows you to ensure that you've answered the important questions and helps prevent paralysis by analysis.

Charlie Isaacs, CTO for Customer Connection & IoT CTO, Salesforce

This book provides a head start for the problem shapers in business by helping to provide context on how we think about the opportunities that lay ahead.

Frank Zeichner, CEO, IoT Alliance Australia & Director, Knowledge Economy Institute, University of Technology Sydney

If you are a director and have not read a book like this then you are failing to prepare - and preparing to fail.

Mark Pesce, Honorary Associate Digital Cultures, University of Sydney Host of The Next Billion Seconds podcast.

Goad and Parker's book is essential reading for modern directors and executives in the disruptive world of IoT. As the allocator of resources, Boards must lead the way in scrutinising all aspects of governance and operations through a digital lens. As the authors say, governance is more than compliance. Modern governance must focus on emerging issues (anticipating, capturing and exploring future opportunities and risks), as well as gaining comfort that today is under control. Boards must redesign their governance frameworks and use the internet to gather positive assurance. IoT should impact the very means by which directors' build, embed and implement good governance. Old ways of governance will not serve new ways of doing business.

This book is a great roadmap to guide problem-shapers in an environment where the only thing that is certain, is uncertainty.

Simon Neaverson, FAICD, Founder of GovernRight™

Today's boards must adapt their strategy in real-time by focusing on the rapid pace of technological change impacting their businesses. The next generation of the internet, specifically the Internet of Things, is already here, and this book compels boards to ask the question "Are we ready?".

Stephen and David have compiled a comprehensive and practical guide for those looking to tackle the complexity of IoT. A #mustread for directors who are not comfortable with having disruption forced upon them, and would rather proactively deliver the strategy needed to transform their businesses before it's too late.

Stuart Waite, CEO, Timpani Board Member, IoT Alliance Australia

Thought leadership is central to our members "value add" to their customers. This book jump starts that process for the Internet of Things

Brett Chalmers, CEO, SMBiTPro

This is a great read. All the things I was most frightened of and least knowledgeable about have been laid bare, and in a language I could actually understand. I am now empowered – IoT, the cloud, AI ,mobility and things Cyber are now within my grasp thanks to Parker and Goad.

Professor Greg Whateley, Executive Dean and Provost, UBSS

When something brand new comes along, it can be difficult to know how to position the opportunity and challenges. This book unravels the right questions and why they are relevant for those facing the new world of IoT.

Dean Calvert, Managing Director, Calvert Technologies

The message of the book is clear: either be disrupted by technological change, or understand how you can transform your business and grow alongside technology. By asking smart questions, Directors can position IoT in the context of their digital workplace and market position before jumping to solution-mode thinking.

Natalie Hardwicke, Digital Workplace Consultant and PhD Candidate

Acknowledgements

No book appears without the support of a considerable number of people both past and present. So, to all of you that have provided the experiences that established the knowledge we have today and those who are still guiding us on the never-ending journey of learning...

THANK YOU

Stephen and David.

Table of Contents

Who should read this book?

Books can be read by many people who will each take away their own version of the story. However, as authors, it is important that we identify a primary audience. This ensures there is clarity in the message we are trying to communicate and a voice that is appropriate.

Primary Audience – Director and Executive as the Problem Shaper

If you are a Director or executive of a medium to large organization that is thinking about what IoT means to your business, then this book is aimed at you.

In writing this book our goal has been to put ourselves in the shoes of Directors at companies where the Internet of Things could have a profound impact on the future of the business. Importantly, we are asking the smart questions that will help in "Problem shaping" not "Problem solving", with a lens of strategy development, policy making, supervision and external accountability (Robert Tricker – Corporate Governance[1]).

What do we mean by "Director"

The term "Director" can have different meanings in a business context. We want to be clear that in the context of this book we are defining Director as:

"A member of the governing board of a business concern who may or may not have an executive function" (Collins Dictionary)

In this context, Directors have legal responsibilities that are defined in a specific jurisdictions company laws (for example The Australian Corporations Act 2001[2] and the UK Companies Act 2006[3])

---

[1] http://www.bobtricker.co.uk/corporate-governance.html

[2] https://www.legislation.gov.au/Details/C2012C00275

[3] http://www.legislation.gov.uk/ukpga/2006/46/pdfs/ukpga_20060046_en.pdf

Secondary Audience – Executive as the Problem Solver

Understanding the questions that a Director is thinking about when they are "Problem shaping", will make it easier for our secondary "Problem solving" audience of Executives as you position your thinking, actions and proposals.

So, whether you are:

- The executive team reporting to the Board of Directors
- An internal project manager charged with delivering IoT solutions
- An external IoT supplier
- Or any other IoT "Problem solver"

We trust you will also find this book useful.

How to use this book

This book is intended to be a catalyst for action. We have structured the book in what we trust is an easy to follow format:

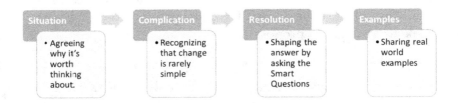

The first two sections (Situation and Complication) are about setting the scene. In the resolution section, we share the Smart Questions that we trust will assist in "problem shaping" the Internet of Things (IoT) opportunity for your organization. Finally, we share some real-world examples that may help give life to all these ideas.

Whilst we believe this flow has merit, please feel free to start wherever you want. You may be con fident about the background to IoT so please jump straight to Chapter 4 and the start of the Smart Questions. Reading the examples first might be the right starting point for you.

Regardless of the order that you read this book, we hope that the ideas and examples inspire you to act. So, do whatever you need to do to make this book useful. Use Post-it notes, write on it, rip it apart, or read it quickly in one sitting. Whatever works for you. We hope this becomes your most dog-eared book.

Chapter 1

Everything and Everywhere

Luck is where opportunity meets preparation.

Seneca (Roman writer, 54 BC – 39 AD)

D IGITAL Transformation is THE buzz phrase wherever you look. It is presented with a "transform or be disrupted" message and rolled up into stories of the 4th industrial revolution[4]. So why is a technology story getting so much air time with Directors and why does it matter?

Imagine a world....

Where your car drops you off at the front door of the office and:

- Carries out a self-diagnostic test and identifies a required repair
- Checks the local service centers for parts availability
- Reviews your diary and asks for your permission to go and be repaired during your 09:30 to 11:30 meeting
- Picks up the children, whose sports day has finished early due to rain, and returns them home
- Asks if you would like it to earn money while it waits for your late meeting to finish by checking for local Uber ride requests.

The technology to allow all these things to happen largely exists today. What is missing is integration, legislation and social

---

[4] *https://www.weforum.org/pages/the-fourth-industrial-revolution-by-klaus-schwab/*

acceptance. But make no mistake these will be addressed and change is coming.

This 4th Industrial revolution is being driven by the four technologies below, however, the business outcomes from this revolution will lead to fundamental and disruptive business change and opportunity. Whilst this book is focused on the Internet of Things (IoT) it should be remembered that IoT is an integral part of this broader picture.

CLOUD
(Compute & Storage Engine)

By 2019 the worldwide public cloud market will have grown to **USD142.2Bn** at 19.4% CAGR[1]

IoT
(Gather Everything)

By 2019 the worldwide IoT market will be USD1.3Tn with **25.6Bn things**. APEJ will dominate with **47.4% revenue share**[3]

AI
(Insights & Actions)

"Cognitive everything." By 2020 over 50% of business analytics software will incorporate **prescriptive analytics**[2]

MOBILE
(Anywhere Access)

By 2020 **2Bn APAC users** will be mobile first[2] By 2018 2m workers will be required to wear health trackers at work[4]

1 - IDC #US40709515 Dec 2015
2 - IDC Futurescape 2016

3 - IDC #US40983216 Feb 2016
4 - Gartner Top Predictions for IT Organisations & Users 2016

- **Internet of Things** – data **gathering** of everything from everywhere
- **Cloud** – on-demand compute and storage **engine**
- **Artificial Intelligence** – learning and **insights**
- **Mobile** – anywhere **access**

There really are only two choices;
- You can take control of you own business transformation
- You can wait until business disruption is forced upon you.

What is this Internet of Things (IoT)

It is widely held that Kevin Ashton coined the phrase "Internet of Things" in 1999[5,6] and described it simply as:

> A system where the Internet is connected to the physical world via ubiquitous sensors

In the consumer world, everyday objects such as watches, phones, fitness trackers, thermostats, TVs, home heating systems, cars and even our pets are being connected to the internet. In the commercial world, trucks, plant equipment, medical devices, and even farm animals are also being connected to the internet. The rapid growth of the Internet of Things has meant that numerous organizations from standards bodies such as the IEEE[7], to commercial software companies such as IBM[8], have worked to establish a more formal definition of IoT.

Our personal choice, because it implies the business value of IoT, is from "The State of Affairs in Internet of Things Research" by Dlodlo N, Foko T, Mvelase P (2012)[9]

> The Internet of Things (IoT) is a set of autonomous devices communicating with each other through the internet with minimal to no human intervention. This communication generates highly useful integrated data about us and the world around us. This data can be acted on in an automated or semi-automated fashion.

---

[5] http://www.rfidjournal.com/articles/view?4986

[6] https://en.wikipedia.org/wiki/Internet_of_things

[7] http://iot.ieee.org/images/files/pdf/IEEE_IoT_Towards_Definition_Internet_of_Things_Revision1_27MAY15.pdf

[8] https://www.ibm.com/internet-of-things/resources/library/what-is-iot/

[9] http://www.ejise.com/issue/download.html?idArticle=829

The Internet of Things (IoT) will change the breadth and depth of data that can be captured on everything in the physical world including human beings. Vast data lakes[10] will provide new insights and enable new processes. Real-time data will allow the proactive automation of actions rather than reactive responses. These insights and actions will revolutionize business.

> Data is the oil of the 21st century and IoT is the untapped reservoir

Governance – a change of focus

A consequence of this is that corporate governance in the form of strategy, policies, supervision and external accountability[11] is going to be impacted and will need to adapt. There will need to be a re-balancing of focus from inward looking, conformance activities (supervisory) to

Bob Tricker, Corporate Governance

outward looking, performance activities (strategy). Reports such as the EY 2017 board priorities for Europe[12] and the US[13] highlight the business impacts of Digital Transformation. All of this sits at the heart of the company Director and problem shapers remit.

> Directors will need to have an increased focus on business strategy

---

[10] https://en.wikipedia.org/wiki/Data_lake

[11] http://www.bobtricker.co.uk/corporate-governance.html

[12] http://www.ey.com/Publication/vwLUAssets/ey-top-priorities-for-european-boards-in-2017/$FILE/EY-top-priorities-for-european-boards-in-2017.pdf

[13] http://www.ey.com/Publication/vwLUAssets/ey-top-priorities-for-us-boards-in-2017/$FILE/ey-top-priorities-for-us-boards-in-2017.pdf

Amazing growth projections

Whilst the ideas of car-sharing and short-term property rental are not new, technology has enabled Uber and Airbnb to provide services at global scale and has fundamentally changed customer experience and disrupted the taxi and hotel industries.

IoT is creating similar changes, which may be less high profile (today), but arguably will have a more widespread impact. There are some amazing short-term predictions for IoT growth:

- According to IDC[14] there will be approximately 3 "things" per person globally, equating to 23Bn+ devices by 2020
- Gartner predict that by 2020 more than 50% of new IT systems will include some form of IoT[15]

This rapid growth is driven in part by the significant technology changes outlined in the diagram above. However other social and regulatory factors have also had a major role to play:

- The broader social shift of the "sharing economy[16]"
- The growing influence of the Millennial generation with their "digital native[17]" attitudes
- Business standards that are no longer fit for purpose in "The age of the customer"[18] (if the taxi industry had been working effectively, would there have been a place for Uber?)
- Regulations and legislation that are struggling to keep up with rapidly changing technology.

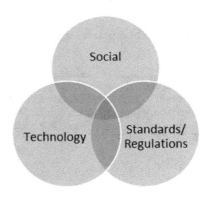

---

[14] http://www.idc.com/getdoc.jsp?containerId=US40983216
[15] http://www.gartner.com/newsroom/id/3185623
[16] https://en.wikipedia.org/wiki/Sharing_economy
[17] https://en.wikipedia.org/wiki/Digital_native
[18] https://go.forrester.com/2017-predictions/

It's already happening

Whilst these are projections, IoT should not be seen as a future opportunity. The market may not yet be mature, but make no mistake IoT is already happening. Below are a few examples.

Digital Twins

"Digital twins[19]" is the idea of capturing data about real world assets and then representing these assets in the virtual world with a digital replica. This allows business to carry out complex real-time monitoring and modeling. This has been identified by Gartner as one of the Top 10 Strategic Technology Trends in 2017[20]. Further, IDC[21] predict that by 2020, 30% of G2000 companies will be using data from digital twins of IoT connected products and assets to improve product innovation success rates and organizational productivity, achieving gains of up to 25%

Lift Manufacturers

Worldwide, problems with lifts (elevators) result in 190 million hours of disruption annually[22]. This results in significant costs and reputational damage for both the manufacturer and the operator. This is leading manufacturers such as Kone[23] and Thyssenkrupp[24] to have major initiatives in the IoT space to transform their maintenance processes from reactive to proactive. As stated:

> "Reports on the elevator's technical condition are transmitted to the cloud for evaluation, providing service engineers with real-time information on necessary repairs and predictions of which specific components will require maintenance, even before the elevator breaks down." **Thyssenkrupp**[25]

---

[19] https://en.wikipedia.org/wiki/Digital_twin

[20] http://www.gartner.com/newsroom/id/3482617

[21] IDC FutureScape: Worldwide IoT 2018 Predictions

[22] https://max.thyssenkrupp-elevator.com/en/

[23] https://www.ibm.com/blogs/internet-of-things/kone/

[24] http://thyssenkrupp-elevator.com.au/en/press_release-17968

[25] https://www.thyssenkrupp.com/en/newsroom/press-releases/press-release-48240.html

---

Aero engines

The high cost of operations and the potentially catastrophic consequences of maintenance failure, means that aero engines provide an ideal use case for data capture and insights through IoT. Rolls Royce[26] have announced a major initiative to use IoT, cloud and AI to reduce fuel costs and provide proactive maintenance.

Industrial Lighting

Lighting in industrial settings can incur high costs due to simple "all on/all off" strategies. Deploying intelligent lighting solutions with sensors to detect movement and ambient lighting conditions allows the optimum light levels to be maintained with the minimum use of artificial lighting. Suppliers such as Vivid Industrial claim savings of 90%+. As stated:

> We are thrilled to announce a whopping 91.7% of energy savings in lighting through the installation of LED lights at Neverfail facility in Peats Ridge. Thanks to our partners Vivid Industrial for a successful roll out! **Coca Cola Amatil**[27]

Smart farming and the Internet of Cows

One area that has gained interest due to its interesting title is the "Internet of Cows". By using GPS, temperature and other IoT sensors, farmers can more actively manage their herds reproductive, health, nutritional and wellbeing status. Companies such as SCR offer a "Cow Intelligence[28]" platform that utilizes cloud, mobile, AI and IoT. As stated:

> "Agriculture is large enough and inefficient enough that there is opportunity for people to come in and improve it" **Todd Dagres, Co-founder Spark Capital (USD3Bn Venture Capitalist)**

---

[26] https://www.rolls-royce.com/media/press-releases/yr-2016/11-07-2016-rr-takes-totalcare-digital-with-microsoft-and-singapore-airlines.aspx

[27] https://www.linkedin.com/feed/update/urn:li:activity:6282741203343548416/

[28] http://www.scrdairy.com/cow-intelligence/cow-intelligence-overview.html

Intelligent shipping containers

If the correct conditions are not maintained during shipping then perishable goods are at risk of damage. Intelligent shipping containers can reduce wastage by actively monitoring and maintaining temperature and humidity conditions[29]. This has additional benefits such as reduced insurance costs.

Drones at refineries

High risk environments such as refineries need to be monitored for potential infrastructure failure. This has traditionally involved complex, high risk and expensive procedures that involve the

shutting down of the area to be inspected. This is a USD40bn annual market and companies such as GE[30] are now using drones and sensors to capture real time data so they can monitor these environments at significantly reduced cost and risk.

Smart cars – driver assist

There is much talk of the self-driving cars of the future. However, even the cars of today have multiple sensors designed to monitor the car and to enhance safety. At the premium end of the market the technology is essentially already self-driving, but due to current legislation, is positioned as diver assist. The latest Audi A8 for example has 41 individual driver-assist systems[31].

[29] *http://ieeexplore.ieee.org/document/6392555/*
[30] *https://inspectioneering.com/news/2017-06-13/6586/ge-begins-testing-drones-to-inspect-refineries-ractories*
[31] *http://www.digit.in/car-tech/the-all-new-audi-a8-has-a-suite-of-41-individual-driver-assist-systems-in-it-35973.html*

We are only limited by our imaginations

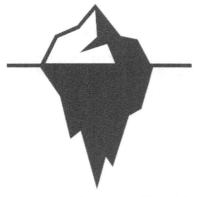

The car is one example of something that is embedded in our daily lives and will undergo massive change. The hype of self-driving cars comes with a strong dose of social skepticism and concern. However, in a world where globally nearly 1.3 million road traffic deaths occur every year, with over 37,000 deaths in the US alone[32], there will be a compelling reason to change. This may well be driven by differential insurance premiums, as the most dangerous part of the car becomes the human driver[33].

This is however only the start. Consider the impact on the taxi industry. Will it be as odd to see a driver in a taxi in 10 years as it would be to see an attendant in an elevator today? What about office design where car parks are no longer required to be "on-site", or whether we even go to an office. What about long term infrastructure planning for roads, railways etc.? Will cars be offered direct from the manufacturers with "uptime" guarantees and contention-ratio rental plans (from "it's all yours" to 1 to 10 shared)? Will un-used cars be made available on "granny-net" to take the aged or infirmed from their house to a local social club or the doctors, with huge social benefits?

> These are only a few ideas, in a single area. New opportunities will be inspired by imagination, not limited by existing knowledge

Inflection point – time for action

We are now at an inflection point where existing market leading businesses will be at risk of disappearing and whole new business

---

[32] http://asirt.org/Initiatives/Informing-Road-Users/Road-Safety-Facts
[33] https://www.businessinsider.com.au/driverless-cars-could-negatively-affect-insurance-industry-2017-2

models will appear. However, this digital transformation must be connected to business transformation and a proactive leadership position for many, would be to work on the basis that:

We are being disrupted. The only question is, do we know about it yet?

Chapter 2

How much changes?

You cannot escape the responsibility of tomorrow by evading it today.

Abraham Lincoln (16th President of the United States, 1809 - 1865)

CHANGE especially when it is radical, can raise fundamental questions about existing "self-evident" truths. We build our strategy and processes around these truths and measure our performance and accountability against them.

Paradoxically, the better we are at performing within the scope of the current axioms the more entrenched our cognitive biases[34] become, and the more difficult it can be to engender change.

Anchoring bias: People are over-reliant on the first piece of information they hear.	**Availability heuristic:** People are over-estimate the importance of information that is available to them.	**Bandwagon effect:** The probability of one person adopting a belief increases based on the number of people who hold that belief.	**Blind-spot bias:** Failing to recognize your own cognitive biases is a bias itself.
Choice-supportive bias: When you choose something, you tend to feel positive about it, even if that has flaws.	**Confirmation bias:** We tend to listen only to information that confirms our preconceptions.	**Conservatism bias:** Where people favour prior evidence over new evidence or information that has emerged.	**Cognitive bias codex:** Summary of dozens of cognitive biases can be found at... https://en.wikipedia.org/wiki/List_of_cognitive_biases

Selection of cognitive biases

---

[34] *https://en.wikipedia.org/wiki/List_of_cognitive_biases*

> **Axiom** [ak-see-uh m], noun, "A statement or proposition which is regarded as being established, accepted, or self-evidently true."
>
> **Axiomatic** [ak-see-uh-mat-ik], adjective, "Self-evident or unquestionable"

Understanding that transformation needs to occur does not mean that it is straight forward. There are always challenges to overcome. However, using these challenges as reasons for only limited action has been the downfall of many businesses over the years.

Kodak[35], Nokia[36] and Pan Am[37] provide examples of how disruptive change in an industry was well signposted, but their leadership was unable to transform the business to take advantage of the opportunity. In the case of Kodak, it was especially ironic that the assets they sold to exit bankruptcy were the patents their own R&D efforts had created for digital imaging.

> The rest of this chapter considers these challenges to change and the consequences of doing nothing

The desire to maintain the status quo

We are told that we now live in a world of constant change, however, for most of the time this is evolutionary not revolutionary. We support the existing strategy by improving our processes, supervising the operations of the business, and enhancing our communications to stakeholders to ensure marketplace confidence.

Visualizing this via the Tricker model of corporate governance[38], in mature

Bob Tricker, Corporate Governance

---

[35] https://hbr.org/2016/07/kodaks-downfall-wasnt-about-technology

[36] https://www.newyorker.com/business/currency/where-nokia-went-wrong

[37] http://www.newsweek.com/pan-american-world-airways-1927-1991-204910

[38] http://www.bobtricker.co.uk/corporate-governance.html

markets Directors will carry out strategy activities, but their focus will normally be in the bottom left and supporting the existing business model (supervisory).

However, in times of change the focus needs to shift to the top right (strategy) and to question the existing norms. This may challenge the skills and operating modes for Directors and problem shapers.

This desire to support the status quo is normal human behavior. Thomas Kuhn in his seminal paper on "The Structure of Scientific Revolutions (1962)"[39] detailed how we are predisposed to support the prevailing model even in the face of apparently overwhelming evidence. Periodically a phase of disruption occurs and a new paradigm[40] becomes accepted. We then re-enter the state of supporting the "new normal".

> To be a truly innovative company[41], innovation needs to be a conscious part of the culture.

Digital literacy

From a "digital" perspective the average age of board members (S&P500, Jan 2015, average age 63.1[42]) typically means that whilst their financial and legal skills are mature, they are less experienced on the technology side. They are certainly not digital natives. There are many reasons for this, a few being:

- IT is still a relatively young discipline. "Computing" only started to be taught in schools in the late 1970's so it is only now that this cohort is entering their 50's
- Technology has for many years been about process improvement and cost management that supports a broader business strategy. It has therefore been left as an Executive responsibility.

[39] https://en.wikipedia.org/wiki/The_Structure_of_Scientific_Revolutions
[40] https://en.wikipedia.org/wiki/Paradigm_shift
[41] https://hbr.org/2015/04/the-5-requirements-of-a-truly-innovative-company
[42] https://www.bloomberg.com/view/articles/2015-01-26/u-s-corporate-directors-are-getting-old

- The business world has often driven technology experts down the "geek" path and not encouraged a balanced business/technology skill set, rendering them less suitable for Board roles

---

Improving digital literacy amongst directors will be a key topic for the nominations and remuneration committee.

The robots are coming – are you ready?

IoT will radically change the way people and businesses operate and interact. It is important to understand from the outset that IoT represents a seismic shift in terms of business models and the way businesses and people will see the world. It is not just about technology or products. People, processes and organizations will be changing because of IoT. Here are just a few examples:

Focus on Outcomes

Perhaps the most profound impact IoT will make on industry is accelerating the shift from selling products and services to selling outcomes. The mass adoption of the internet and the social shift from ownership to utilization of assets has seen a shift to outcomes from products and features. The increasing emergence of IoT will accelerate this evolution. Consumers will no longer purchase a car, they will simply pay to get from "A to B". Industrial manufacturers will not want to purchase replacement parts for their equipment, they will expect the parts suppliers to simply sell machine uptime. Farmers will not call a veterinarian when one of their animals is sick, they will expect to pay a fee per animal, based on the healthiness of the animal throughout the year. There is significant profit to be made by the vendors of these services and solutions as they can bundle many components together to provide the customer with an outcome. But it also means a transfer of risk, which the business providing the service may not be capable (or willing) of undertaking with their current business models.

There will be a shift from buyer beware to supplier beware

Everything as a Service

The "as-a-Service" model has been the emerging model of the software industry over the last 5 years. This business model has meant great success for some companies but has been the cause of significant challenges for others, who have not been able to adapt. In the "as-a-Service" model the provider takes on the risk of service delivery and typically only gets paid if the service is available. This model connects with the growing desire for both people and businesses to have access to the use of an asset rather than the ownership. Breaking the CAPEX constraint means more people are able to access services that were traditionally the domain of Enterprise customers only. Connecting everything to the internet now enables everything to be as-a-Service and aligns to the focus on outcomes. We have seen reductions in computer server sales with virtualization and cloud adoption[43]. Will we see, for example, the same for car sales as people increasingly rent or car-share. How will self-driving cars impact utilization?

> Everywhere you look people are experimenting with "as-a-Service" models – what are your plans?

AI and robots

The combination of real time data from IoT devices, with unconstrained compute and storage services, will allow AI services to make human-like decisions. There are potentially huge efficiencies to be gained where manual checks can be avoided and the cycles of reporting, approval, and validation can be compressed. Phrases such as Smart Cities,

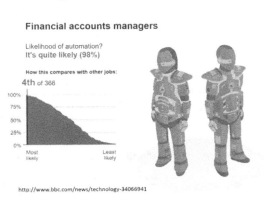

Financial accounts managers

Likelihood of automation?
It's quite likely (98%)

How this compares with other jobs:
4th of 366

http://www.bbc.com/news/technology-34066941

---

[43] https://www.comparethecloud.net/news/gartner-says-worldwide-server-shipments-declined-4-2/

How much changes?

Smart Offices and Smart Countryside are used, but they all involve some form of IoT and smart analytics.

> Many traditional process roles will be automated and with AI, even previously "skilled" roles will be challenged. Is this a headcount reduction or redeployment to higher value roles?

New Revenue models

Business is still business. However, the advent of the internet has seen existing models become profitable at scale and new models emerge. Google demonstrated the power of advertising ($79.38Bn in 2016[44]), eBay the power of transaction fees through the two-sided market place ($2.3Bn revenue for Q2FY17[45]). IoT will deliver opportunities to reconsider other existing models. Will smart lights with movement and ambient light level sensors allow for payment based on maintaining an agreed light level rather than selling the light bulbs themselves? Will hotels pay for elevators by the hours of usage and maintenance companies be penalized if an engineer is required during working hours? Crucially the money only flows with ongoing customer satisfaction.

Risk transfers through the channel to the customer

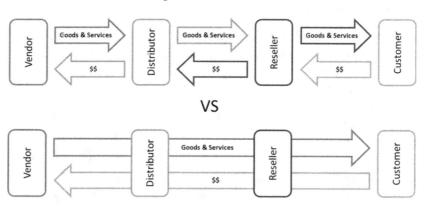

Risk retained by the channel, payment for ongoing satisfaction

> These models will require customer centric rather than product centric thinking.

[44] https://www.statista.com/statistics/266249/advertising-revenue-of-google/
[45] https://www.ebayinc.com/stories/news/ebay-inc-reports-second-quarter-2017-results/

Monetization of the Data Stream

As the old saying goes "knowledge is power" and the vast amounts of data that IoT devices will collect, creates an opportunity to create new knowledge. Effectively monetizing this will be a key success metric. A 2015 survey by Tata Consulting Services suggested that 47.7% of "IoT leaders" had changed their business models to drive revenue from customer usage data, compared to only 20% of "IoT followers"[46]. Is the real value of Fitbit[47] the revenue from the devices it sells or the vast amount of personalized data it now holds?

> The challenge will be ensuring that this monetization opportunity is not abused. This will require businesses and governments to establish ethical guidelines.

Increased Personalization and Context

Highly customized and personalized content will be the way of the future. Observe a digital native[48] and you will see a short attention span that surfs content almost continuously. To be effective, content must be timely, specific and contextual. IoT promises to multiply the effect as we have more of a view as to where people are and what they are doing before we communicate with them.

> Failure to maintain security around this personalized data could have significant legal and reputational consequences.

New Experiences Created Through Information Convergence

By combining information from a number of sources people's experiences will become more optimized. This means that companies will need to work together more and that people's expectations will increase. Combining data from your travel

---

[46] *https://www.forbes.com/sites/louiscolumbus/2015/07/28/where-internet-of-things-initiatives-are-driving-revenue-now/*
[47] *http://www.fitbit.com*
[48] *https://en.wikipedia.org/wiki/Digital_native*

booking services, your health tracker and social media feeds of your network may alert you and the health services to the spread of contagious diseases.

What new partnerships do you need to accelerate the value of the data you possess?

Social and Commercial Transparency

It used to be that information was essentially private by default and we chose to share it. Reports were stored in a filing cabinet or a private server. Photographs were rarely taken on "nights out" and even if they were taken then they would be printed and put in a photo album at home. Now it is the opposite, we need to assume that information will be generally available and effort will be required to retain privacy. Businesses share data electronically making it easier to pass on. Camera phones mean photos can be captured and shared with global audiences without context or permission. This transparency will mean that our actions both individually and as businesses will be increasingly visible. This could have profound impacts for some.

Data that is anonymous alone may become identifiable when mashed up with other data sources. What protections do you need to put in place?

Proactive Prediction of Real and Emergent Needs

A consequence of mass adoption of IoT and the changes outlined above will be a greater ability to predict the future. Whether it be elevator maintenance, car servicing or even our own health, the vast data lakes combined with smart analytics (Artificial Intelligence) will offer both real time insights and predictions for the future. From the person whom enters a retail store and is immediately presented with sale offers based on previous purchase history to the multimillion dollar mining earth mover that is proactively taken offline to have its transmission oil replaced because the transmission temperature has been increasing.

> What real time insights and future predictions will enhance the short and long-term profitability of your business?

Longer Product Life Cycles with Over the Air Updates

Most devices from your car, your TV to you clothes washer, are an agglomeration of physical hardware and software. Just like the operating system of your desktop these devices connected to the internet are capable of over-the-air updates. On the one hand, this means that new features and functions can be seamlessly added to the device to add value. On the other hand, this will contribute to people using things longer, ultimately having an impact on a company's product revenue stream.

> How will you drive customer centric value from enhanced services that can be offered through your product footprint?

Ecosystems will be the cornerstone

The delivery of IoT solutions requires many different components from the Thing itself, to the hardware, communications infrastructure, systems integration, databases to store the data, technologies to extract and manipulate the data, artificial intelligence to create information and drive actions and services to operate the systems. Taken together no one industry player can provide all the components of an IoT solution. This means that both the industry players and their customers will need to get used to managing an increasingly complex variety of partnerships.

> Who will you partner with to achieve your desired outcomes? Are you current suppliers (internal and external) fit for purpose?

Inaction brings its own risks

Despite business opportunities, we are still at an early stage of mass deployment. Legislation, standards, business models and tools are still emerging in the IoT space. However, as previously mentioned, IoT is already happening and may be part of your business without either conscious planning or awareness of the risks. Businesses need to engage now to proactively adapt to this change. Failure to do so may expose businesses to the possibility of:

Corporate liability

IoT hacking nearly damaged a German steel mill[49] (with a risk of corporate manslaughter), the FDA recently recalled a web connected pacemaker with the ability to be hacked (with the risk of reputational liability)[50], an attack at the heart of the internet (DynDNS) was launched via poor security on internet connected DVRs and video cameras[51] (with the risk of commercial liability). Do these exposures impact Director liability?

Privacy liability

IoT will provide vast amounts of contextual information and increase social and commercial transparency. But what will the privacy implications be? Sharing our health data allows the ambulance to arrive before we are ill, but what privacy issues occur to achieve this? How will this increased transparency affect your business?

> Will informed consent at point of collection be sufficient or will we require new frameworks for consent at point of use?

Business viability

Supply chain disintermediation can lead to whole business models and job roles (especially those providing "man in the middle" services) being at risk from IoT. Are you or your business at risk?

---

[49] *https://securityintelligence.com/german-steel-mill-meltdown-rising-stakes-in-the-internet-of-things/*

[50] *https://www.engadget.com/2017/01/09/fda-warns-that-certain-pacemakers-are-vulnerable-to-hacking/*

[51] *https://krebsonsecurity.com/2016/10/hacked-cameras-dvrs-powered-todays-massive-internet-outage/*

Market valuation

In the IT industry, 'Everything as a Service' has caused transformational change from upfront to subscription revenue. This will impact other industries as the cost of IoT drops and more assets become internet connected, facilitating EaaS business models. How will these changes in revenue model impact your market valuation?

Adoption timing risk

Early in the IoT adoption cycle technology risks (such as security and reliability) are high due to the immaturity of the IoT solutions being deployed and the inexperience of the organizations deploying them. But the total risk exposure to a corporation is less due to the general lack of adoption with fewer and a lower variety of IoT endpoints having been deployed. At later stages, increased adoption with an increasing number and variety of IoT endpoints deployed increases the risk exposure to the company. However. enhanced technology maturity and the increased experience the business has with deploying IoT technology begins to reduce risk. Paradoxically then, the greatest corporate risk is not at the beginning or the later stages of the IoT technology adoption cycle, but rather in the middle where product maturity and the business experience with IoT has not overcome the impact of increased IoT adoption. This could mean that the highest risk for your company is yet to come. Where is your business on this curve?

Inaction could mean that IoT leaves you and your business exposed to risks and potential obsolescence.

IoT is not just "New IT"

The business use of Information technology has evolved rapidly and constantly since the mass commercial availability of IT systems in the 1960s[52]. During this time, there have been significant changes as we have shifted from centralized mainframes to distributed networks and more recently to cloud computing. IoT is bringing another shift, however, there are such key differentiators that it will not be possible to just take existing IT thinking and apply this to IoT.

Traditional IT	IoT
Driven by rapidly *increasing capability* for the same or similar cost (linked to Moore's Law[53]). High quality focus.	Focus on *cost reduction* to attain ubiquity of use, with consequence of resources diverted away from "advanced" features such as security.
Mature market. Well established industry leaders and supplier ecosystems. Mature and commonly adopted standards.	*Emerging market.* Key vendors have only recently released their IoT offerings[54]. Of the 34 technologies identified in the 2016 Gartner IoT Hype Cycle[55] only 2 are identified as less than 2 years to mainstream adoption. Standards are emerging and not commonly adopted.

---

[52] *https://en.wikipedia.org/wiki/IBM_System/360*
[53] *https://en.wikipedia.org/wiki/Moore%27s_law*
[54] *https://www.gartner.com/doc/3086918/market-guide-iot-platforms*
[55] *https://www.gartner.com/doc/3371743/hype-cycle-internet-things-*

Traditional IT	IoT
CIO = Chief Information **Officer**. Heads of IT have typically been hired to improve service quality and drive down costs in relatively well understood environments, all in the context of flat budgets.	*CIO* = Chief *Innovation* **Officer**. IoT will require creative thinking within immature environments. Where significant new benefits can be found, new budgets will be allocated.
Architectural *homogeneity*. A limited set of mature platforms (e.g. Windows, Unix/Linux, IoS and Android) allowing easy access to resources (people and technology).	Architectural *heterogeneity*. Multiple commercially available platforms, potentially hundreds of regionally developed. Leading to complexity in delivering end to end solutions.
Highly controlled deployment environments. Typically known locations, reliable power and connectivity, mature support and security services.	*Limited control* deployment environments. Typically, in remote and often hostile environments. Minimal compute, storage and limited (battery) power (restricting services such as firewall, anti-virus). With intermittent/low power connectivity.
Limited support reach and Reactive – support is typically limited to small numbers of "experts" who are approved to call support services in the event of a problem, which in turn elicits a "reactive" response.	*Vastly extended support reach and proactive* – vast numbers of IoT devices will provide data in near real time about their status. AI analysis will then auto-generate proactive support calls. Support, parts and rostering systems will need to be able to auto-respond to these requests.

Evolutionary thinking and processes will not allow you gain maximum value from the IoT opportunity.

What next?

Change is always coming, but the 4th industrial revolution is creating a threat and an opportunity for businesses around the world. IoT is a foundational piece of the technology puzzle that is driving these changes. We are not yet at a highly mature point in the adoption cycle and government legislation, privacy rules and social maturity are still catching up. However, there is sufficient momentum to ensure that this needs to be on the Directors and problem shapers agenda.

Even though there are challenges, failure to act will mean that investors as well as the wider stakeholder community will hold you to account.

Chapter

3

Ask the Smart Questions

If I have seen further it is by standing on the shoulders of giants

Isaac Newton (Scientist, 1643 – 1727)

SMART Questions is about giving you valuable insights or "the Smarts". Normally these are only gained through years of painful and costly experience. Whether you already have a general understanding of the subject and need to take it to the next level or are starting from scratch, you need to make sure you ask the Smart Questions. We aim to short circuit that learning process, by providing the expertise of the 'giants' that Isaac Newton referred to.

We do not expect all the questions to be new or insightful to all readers. The value you get will clearly vary and depend on your previous experience. However, if you apply the 3Rs then we believe that all the questions will have some value.

The 3 Rs

Some of the questions will be in areas where you know the answers already so the book will **Reinforce** them in your mind.

You may have forgotten some aspects of the subject, so the questions will **Remind** you.

Other questions may **Reveal** new insights to you that you've never considered before.

How do you use Smart Questions?

The structure of the questions is set out in Chapter 4, and the questions are in Chapters 5 through 7. The questions are laid out in a series of structured and ordered tables with the questions in one column and the explanation of why it matters alongside. We've also provided a checkbox so that you can mark which questions are relevant to your situation.

A quick scan down the first column in the list of questions should give you a general feel of where you are for each question vs. the 3Rs. At the highest level, they are a sanity check or checklist of areas to consider.

In Chapter 8 we have tried to bring some of the questions to life with some real-life examples.

We trust that you will find real insights. There may be some "aha" moments. Hopefully not too many sickening, head in the hands "what have we done' moments. Even if you do find yourself in such a situation, the questions may help you to re-establish some order, take control, and steer yourself back into calmer waters.

In this context, probably the most critical role of the Smart Questions is to reveal risks that you might not have considered. On the flipside, they should also open your thinking to opportunities that haven't yet occurred to you. Balancing the opportunities and the risks, and then agreeing what is realistically achievable is the key to formulating an effective strategy.

How to dig deeper

Need more information? Not convinced by the examples, or want ones that are more relevant to your specific situation? Why not contact the Authors? They are, after all, the domain experts whose knowledge has raised your interest. For more details contact Smart Questions at *info@smart-questions.com* or the authors directly at *david.goad@sydney.edu.au* and *stephen@smart-questions.com*.

And finally

Please remember that these questions are NOT intended to be a prescriptive list that must be followed slavishly from beginning to end. It is also inevitable that the list of questions is not exhaustive and we are confident that with the help of the community the list of Smart Questions will grow.

If you want to rephrase a question to improve its context or have identified a question we've missed, then let us know to add to the collective knowledge (*feedback@smart-questions.com*)

We also understand that not all the questions will apply to all businesses. However, we encourage you to read them all as there may be a nugget of truth that can be adapted to your circumstances.

Above all we do hope that it provides a guide or a pointer to the areas that may be valuable to you and helps with the "3 Rs".

Problem Shaping Questions

If I had an hour to solve a problem I'd spend 55 minutes thinking about the problem and 5 minutes thinking about solutions.

Albert Einstein (Theoretical Physicist. 1879 – 1955)

THERE are 170 Smart Questions in this book, but they can all be summarised by three top-level questions. Everyone who is even beginning to think about the Internet of Things and the potential for business transformation should be able to address each of these three critical areas confidently. You need to ask yourself:

Chapter 5: Are we ready?

1. What is motivating us?
2. Organisational readiness.

Chapter 6: What will change?

1. What parts of our business strategy change?
2. How does your business model change?
3. What people, process and technology changes occur?
4. How are your external stakeholders impacted?

Chapter 7: What is involved with delivering an IoT strategy?

1. Implementation partners
2. Technology infrastructure
3. Security and privacy

Each of these three top-level Smart Questions is addressed in the following chapters. Within each chapter, you will find more detailed sets of Smart Questions, which explore that topic. These are designed to help you shape an outcome that is tailored to your specific circumstances. Each section and sub-section deals with a specific topic, so feel free to dip into specific areas of interest or work through the questions top to bottom – whatever works for you.

Chapter

Are we ready?

You can't cross the sea merely by standing and staring at the water.

Rabindranath Tagore (Author and polymath, 1861 – 1941)

C HANGE is difficult and maintaining the status quo is often seen as the easier and more prudent option. However, as discussed in the previous chapters, the forces of change are so powerful now that there really are only two choices:

- Take control of you own business transformation
- Wait until business disruption is forced upon you

Being clear about the factors that will motivate the timing for you to act and the readiness of your organization to engage in change could fundamentally alter the risks and the degree of control associated with your business transformation.

Have you lost business? Will IoT enable you to capture or defend a market? Is it being demanded of you by customers? Is the business culture ready for change?

Be clear about these drivers or goals as they will inform your other questions.

5.1 Motivation

At a personal level, most of us will have experienced the dilemma of knowing we need to change something in our lives, but without the correct motivation it seems impossible to do. You know you need to get fitter, lose weight or move on from your current job, but we convince ourselves we will get to it tomorrow.

Businesses are run by people and so these human traits become blockers for business change. Understanding the motivations that have led you to be "Thinking of…IoT from the Director's perspective?" is the critical first part of the journey.

☒	Question	Why this matters
☐	5.1.1 Have you lost business because you did not have an IoT strategy?	There is no more compelling reason to consider alternative approaches than when you are actively losing business.
☐	5.1.2 Is there pressure from your customers to explore IoT solutions?	Even if you have not lost business directly, your customers may be reviewing their IoT options. Are you being proactive and engaging with them?
☐	5.1.3 Are the industry analysts for your sector predicting that now is the right time for an IoT strategy?	Arguably the first safe time to invest is when the analysts for your sector are predicting that IoT is ready now. Although you will have missed the early adopter position you will have also avoided some of the potential risks. As always there is a fine balance and each business will have their own style that will determine where this balance point is.
☐	5.1.4 Would your reputation for being a market innovator suffer without a IoT strategy?	You may have built your reputation based on always being on the leading edge. Being late to market could impact this reputation. However, as with any emerging market, timing is everything.
☐	5.1.5 Are you perceived as conservative and want to add a little edge to your offering?	Investing in IoT could create marketing opportunities to establish your business as a thought leader. As long as this is aligned to true business benefits it may drive value with your stakeholders.

☒	Question	Why this matters
☐	5.1.6 Are your existing competitors investing in IoT?	Just as you are now thinking about the IoT, it is likely that your competitors are as well and you need to be positioned to respond with a compelling story that explains your position in this space.
☐	5.1.7 Are new businesses entering your market and using IoT as a disruptive strategy?	One of the reasons for considering IoT is it creates opportunities to reduce costs, extend geographically, and monetize vertical business process expertise. Unfortunately, just as this is good for you, it also creates opportunities for others to extend into your market. One of the challenges here is that you may not even be aware that these businesses exist, never mind the new reality that they are competitors
☐	5.1.8 Can you increase the barriers to entry for potential competitors?	Being seen as having a clear IoT strategy may in itself enhance the market's perception of you. It may be part of your business model to be seen as leading edge. It may also send a clear signal to the existing and new competitors that are entering your market that you intend to lead in the IoT space.
☐	5.1.9 Could you gain first mover advantages by investing in IoT?	A first mover advantage has the potential to make your competitors' strengths irrelevant by providing customers with something so different that you change the game.
☐	5.1.10 Is this an opportunity to drive innovation?	Are there current ways of working which could be changed dramatically with IoT? Innovation is the driver for future revenue and/or longer-term cost savings.

☒	Question	Why this matters
☐	5.1.11 What expansion can you achieve without incurring additional cost?	Will you be able to offer more for less because of an IoT approach? Are there areas where your expansion is being limited? Are the expansion opportunities geographical, product, operational/support or financial?
☐	5.1.12 Does IoT present a Blue Ocean Strategy[56] opportunity?	A Blue Ocean Strategy has at its heart the notion of making your competitors strengths irrelevant by providing the customer with something so different that you change the game.
☐	5.1.13 Is your reputation being damaged due to poor service levels?	Being stuck in a broken elevator with nothing to look at but the manufacturer's name. Seeing a truck with your company name, broken down at the side of the road. Being in the news for another unplanned service disruption. IoT could provide the insights that prevent these risks to your reputation.
☐	5.1.14 Will IoT help transform your support costs?	Can IoT provide insights into your business operations that could radically transform the costs of support? For example, remote sensing could ensure an engineer is sent onsite "just in time", saving costs and potentially reputational damage.
☐	5.1.15 Do you need to reduce your operational costs?	The IoT allows you to improve operational efficiencies and reduce operational costs. Examples include elimination of job roles required for monitoring and preventive maintenance and more process automation leading to less administration cost.

---

[56] *Blue Ocean Strategy* by W. Chan Kim & Renee Mauborgne

☒	Question	Why this matters
☐	5.1.16 Do you need to improve your customer intimacy?	IoT will allow you to collect more information about your customers and the environment they operate in. This will provide greater insights and facilitate amongst other things: • proactive rather than reactive activities • tailored selling outcomes
☐	5.1.17 Do you need to improve your responsiveness?	IoT allows you to reduce time to market. IoT connected customers can provide near real time data on their requirements. For example, Amazon's Dash[57] allows customer to order new products with the touch of a button as soon as they run out.
☐	5.1.18 Do you need to drive more annuity revenue streams?	IoT enables as-a-Service business models. Already commercial photocopies are billed on a per copy basis. As the cost of IoT decreases lower cost capital assets can be charged on an as-a-Service basis. For example, a home dishwasher that is charged on a per wash basis.
☐	5.1.19 Are you concerned about exposures with existing unplanned or unknown IoT deployments?	It is highly likely that you already have some IoT infrastructure within your organization. Without good network and infrastructure monitoring tools you may not even be aware of this. Understanding what is already out there will allow for appropriate risk management to be put in place.

---

[57] *https://www.amazon.com/Dash-Buttons/b?ie=UTF8&node=10667898011*

5.2 Organizational readiness

Being motivated is one thing, but bringing the rest of the company with you on the journey of change can be a different story. Business history is littered with companies who understood change was required but for various reasons could not or would not act. For  example, Kodak sold their substantial portfolio of digital imaging patents as part of the process to exit bankruptcy[58].

It will be easy for businesses to use external factors that are "beyond their control" to delay change. However, for many the reality will be a lack of internal organizational readiness. Culture, skills, supply chain relationships and economic and legal drivers within the current and future business are just a few of the potential banana skins on the path to change.

There are significant technology questions that need to be asked but we get to those later. This section is about your organizations readiness to change.

---

[58] *http://www.nytimes.com/2012/12/20/business/kodak-to-sell-patents-for-525-million.html*

☒	Question	Why this matters
☐	5.2.1 What image about change are the Board and CEO projecting?	As with all major changes, success is directly linked to clear support from the senior leaders of the business.
☐	5.2.2 How clearly is the "Why" of businesses understood?	Ensuring the why or the purpose of the company is clearly and consistently communicated internally and externally will ensure there is an overriding guiding light during the change process.
☐	5.2.3 Have you conducted a change readiness assessment of your organization?	Seeking input from your employees will help you understand their readiness for change and how you can help them through the change.
☐	5.2.4 Have you included your IoT strategy into your 3 to 5 year plan?	IoT can have such broad reaching impacts on business it is important that your overall business strategy accounts for this.
☐	5.2.5 Have the necessary investment budgets been set aside for your IoT Strategy?	IoT will become a material part of everyone's IT budget. You will need a strategy to make the most of your IoT investments.
☐	5.2.6 Have you developed an IoT specific Security Strategy?	The volume and unique characteristics of IoT deployments create new opportunities for cyber threats. Who is responsible for this and the related strategy?

☒	Question	Why this matters
☐	5.2.7 Do you have a privacy strategy?	IoT increases the volumes of potentially private data collected about individuals. New privacy legislation potentially increases your corporate liability.
☐	5.2.8 Do you have the right skills amongst the current Directors to shape the IoT strategy?	There may be a need to enhance the digital literacy skills of the current Boards, to add new Directors and to provide expert board advisory resources
☐	5.2.9 When was the last time you did a skills review across the company?	IoT initiatives require a number of skill sets to be successful. Have you identified those skills within the organization and if not, how will you acquire them (internal hiring or external partners)?
☐	5.2.10 Do job descriptions and responsibilities, even at the most senior level, need to be updated?	Is the CIO a Chief information or Innovation officer? These roles require different skills.
☐	5.2.11 Are there requirements for net new senior roles within the business?	The increased capture and processing of information may require roles such as Chief Privacy Office and Chief Security Officer to be introduced. To provide the appropriate segregation these may need to sit outside the IT operational team.

☒	Question	Why this matters
☐	5.2.12 Do you have a change management strategy for the roles that will change or be eliminated through IoT?	With the potential for changes in job roles and responsibilities through IoT people will need assistance to navigate through this change. A culture of loyalty to staff can create challenges if it is necessary to let staff go.
☐	5.2.13 Is ongoing learning and training part of the company culture?	The disruptive nature of IoT will likely mean new skills will be required, whether these be new business processes or use of new applications. If staff are used to ongoing training then it will be easier to get them up to speed with the new skills.
☐	5.2.14 How effective is your process for onboarding new staff?	New employees may be required to address skills shortages. Having an efficient onboarding process will minimize disruption.
☐	5.2.15 Are internal champions involved and supportive?	Some of your best current business champions can be the largest blockers. Change represents a potential shift in their status within the business and their perceived ability to be successful going forward.
☐	5.2.16 How are new ideas and opinions heard within the business?	Internal listening will assist in maintaining motivation during the inevitable business changes ahead.

☒	Question	Why this matters
☐	5.2.17 Do you have a partner strategy for your IoT initiatives?	You will need several partners to support you in the development of IoT. Contrary to what a technology provider may tell you, most Systems Integrators or Technology providers don't have the capability to provide you with a full IoT solution. You will need to have a number of partners and you will need to make sure that those partners can work together.
☐	5.2.18 Do you have an IoT Platform Strategy?	There are at least 16 available IoT platforms. Gartner indicates that the average business will have at least two different IoT Platforms by 2020. A large proportion of IoT budgets will be spent on integration. Many IoT technologies risk becoming obsolete. Selection of the most appropriate IoT platform, that achieves the balance of your IoT needs, whilst minimizing the potential for obsolescence, will be key to reducing your IoT investment costs.
☐	5.2.19 What is your current relationship with external stakeholders?	You may need to enhance these relationships so you can keep them abreast of the changes you are making to the business and hence avoid any "surprised" reactions.
☐	5.2.20 Have you developed a communications plan?	It will be critical to have a coordinated strategy for communicating any change initiative to both internal and external stakeholders.

☒	Question	Why this matters
☐	5.2.21 Are there external parties that will need to be notified for compliance purposes?	The changes you are planning may be material enough to be part of your "continuous disclosure" obligations. There may be compliance organizations who need to be made aware of a change in data that you are capturing and storing.
☐	5.2.22 When was the last time you carried out a Customer Satisfaction Survey?	Listening to your customers will provide a benchmark and ability to track the effectiveness of the changes being put in place.
☐	5.2.23 What existing projects need to be expanded, merged, amended or stopped?	There will be existing projects already in process. Understanding how they support your IoT strategy will allow you to effectively plan ongoing and future investments in these projects.
☐	5.2.24 Do you have clarity about the existing IT infrastructure?	You may be able to re-use existing infrastructure or understand where there will be deployment challenges.
☐	5.2.25 Do you have a business risk management process that also covers IT systems?	Changing legislation increases the need to demonstrate awareness, compliance and reporting of any systems risks. Risk management needs to be owned at the highest level.

☒	Question	Why this matters
☐	5.2.26 How well understood and documented is the "Customer Journey"?	Technology and economic forces have put an increasing amount of control in the hands of the customer. ("Digital Transformation In The Age Of The Customer"59). Understanding the complete sum of experiences that customers go through when interacting with your company and brand will be crucial in understanding how and where IoT can be used to enhance their journey.
☐	5.2.27 Are there existing contracts with customers that could impact your IoT plans?	Customer contracts may need to be reviewed and possibly altered or re-negotiated to reflect changes to information acquisition, storage and analysis.
☐	5.2.28 Are there commercial relationships with existing technology suppliers that could impact your IoT plans?	Long term supply contracts with existing technology providers could create lock-ins that are expensive to exit.
☐	5.2.29 What is the value of current infrastructure in your accounts?	Some existing infrastructure investments may carry forward. Others may no longer be fit for purpose. What impact would financial write-downs have on your decision-making process?

---

59 *https://www.accenture.com/_acnmedia/Accenture/Conversion-Assets/DotCom/Documents/Global/PDF/Digital_2/Accenture-Digital-Transformation-In-The-Age-Of-The-Customer.pdf*

☒	Question	Why this matters
☐	5.2.30 Are there tax or accounting benefits available for IoT projects?	Governments around the world recognize the need to encourage digital transformation. In line with this they offer incentives to encourage investment. For example, Australia offers R&D tax incentives60.

60 https://www.business.gov.au/assistance/research-and-development-tax-incentive

Chapter 6

What changes?

It always seems impossible until it's done

Nelson Mandela (Politician, 1918 – 2013)

IT is clear that new technologies lead to new business models, new business strategies and often whole new businesses. One only has to look at history for examples of this. The steam engine lead to mass production and the 1st industrial revolution. The advent of the internet led to proliferation of whole new business such as eBay, Facebook and Amazon. The relationship between technology and change has been well documented in the academic literature.[61] It is hard to see the future and predict what changes will happen particularly given the breadth and depth of change that IoT could lead to. It is easier to observe the market factors that are driving the change and then to ask how this will impact your businesses strategy, business model and

---

[61] Baden-Fuller, C., & Haefliger, S. (2013). Business models and technological innovation. Long range planning, 46(6), 419-426.

the people and operations that support that business model.

To have this discussion we need to take a moment to discuss the relationship between business strategy, business models and business operations (people and processes).

There are whole books and academic articles written on the definitions of the three terms business strategy, business models and business operations and there is some debate on the exact definition of each. For the purposes of this discussion, let's keep the definitions and discussion simple and illustrate with a few examples. Simply put if the Business Strategy is the "What" of the business, then the Business Model is the "How", and the Organization is the "Who" (the resources of people, processes, technology, etc.) that supports the business model which in turn supports the business strategy.

Take eBay for example. One might say that their business strategy is to become the number one online retail market. Their business model is to provide a two-sided market with buyers on one hand and sellers on the other taking a transaction fee on every transaction. Organizationally they provide the website, development teams, and associated customer support along with the search engine optimization and marketing of the website. Overall, these elements attract buyers to the seller's electronic store fronts, and technology tools like PayPal are used to support electronic payments.

Another example might be the Android Operating System (OS) owned by Google on your mobile phone. Google might say that their business strategy was to become the number one technology platform for mobile phones. Their business model could be described as a platform provider in which they build very little additional functionality themselves, but encourage businesses to develop applications on their operating system to provide that functionality. Google then takes a commission from the sale of the applications made by the developers. The organization of Google would therefore be designed to support the recruitment of those application developers, providing them with training and a rich development platform, and ecommerce traction platform to facilitate selling of those applications.

You might argue about the specifics of the business strategy, business model and associated business organization in these two examples. However, the point was to convey an understanding of the three concepts to allow you to answer for yourself the questions of what is your business strategy, business model and organization in this new world of IoT. Once that is done you can then ask the questions about how your key stakeholders will be impacted by those business strategy, business model and organizational changes.

6.1 Business strategy changes

We talked in preceding chapters about the large number of ways that businesses can be impacted from the Internet of Things. The core impact of IoT will be a change from selling physical products and services to selling outcomes as-a-Service. As a result, there will be a transfer of risk from customers to vendors as vendors are expected to take on more responsibility resulting from supply chain disintermediation, greater customer intimacy and a subscription model that re-enforces payment based on satisfaction not just supply.

There is a precedent for this level of change and it is the software industry. In the last five years the move to the cloud and as-a-Service models has been one of the most significant changes in IT. We have seen three broad scenarios:

- New businesses that have emerged during this era becoming multi-billion dollar revenue organizations e.g. Salesforce
- Businesses that have pivoted to the new model, retaining their market leading position e.g. Microsoft
- Businesses that have lost their way and have struggled under the as-a-Service model. There are several examples of this in the IT hardware industry.

As IoT connects the physical world to the virtual one and the changes we've seen in IT begin to impact other industries, it will be critical for those industries to ask themselves if their business strategy needs to change and whether "what" they sell is likely to be changing from a product or service to an outcome. If that change is going to happen then it will be critical for them to get ahead of the change to manage the transition to their new strategy.

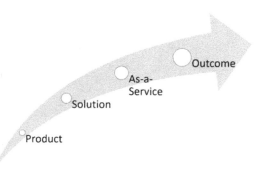

☒	Question	Why this matters
☐	6.1.1 How well do you understand your customer's needs?	IoT provides increased visibility of customer activity and preference which facilitates more targeted sales and marketing and may lead to significant product re-alignment and re-engineering opportunities.
☐	6.1.2 Does your business provide distribution or services as an intermediary for other businesses?	IoT provides the ability to connect end users directly to the service providers. This creates the potential for increased customer intimacy but may also eliminate businesses that have served this intermediary function for a manufacturer.
☐	6.1.3 Does your customer change with IoT?	IoT provides the ability to connect end users directly to the service providers. This may mean that instead of selling to a distributer you are selling to an end customer.
☐	6.1.4 Do you provide large capital assets? Are those capital assets usually paid as a single upfront price?	IoT has the ability to enable "Everything as a Service Business Models". As-a-Service models are great because most shareholder's value consistent revenue streams. But initial profitability can drop as the revenue from sales is spread over several years.
☐	6.1.5 Will IoT enable you to sell your product "as-a-Service"	Everything-as-a-Service may change your business profitability model. IoT can enable you to sell a more comprehensive solution. For example, instead of paying for the car up front, IoT connected cars enable the user to be charged on a per use basis. Maintenance services and real-time customer service can be included in the bundle (as the car can be monitored remotely).

☒	Question	Why this matters
☐	6.1.6 Does your business provide post-sales support to your customers?	IoT enables automation of post-sales support and service. Internet connected instrumentation and equipment can automatically identify maintenance issues and alert the vendor to send service staff to resolve the issue (e.g. an elevator that has a vibration sensor which indicates one of its bearings is at risk of imminent failure). This can provide a point of differentiation for customers.
☐	6.1.7 Does your business provide consumables that need to be regularly replenished for your customers?	IoT enables supply chain automation (fleet management, route optimization, warehouse inventory), semi-automation (e.g. Amazon's Dash) 62 and therefore increased replenishment velocity.
☐	6.1.8 Do the products you sell have a software component?	IoT enables regular over-the-air technology updates which means the life cycle of the product extends and new capabilities can be delivered as you go. It also potentially represents a decrease in services activities as more issues may be solved remotely.
☐	6.1.9 Does moving to an outcome based strategy mean more of an industry focus?	Selling outcomes can mean that you are selling something that is more industry specific which means your strategy should be more industry focused. For example, instead of selling parts that go into large agricultural equipment you begin to sell the outcome which is equipment uptime. This means that you are dealing more with the end customer and depending on the type of agriculture they are doing the uptime requirements could be different.

---

62 *https://www.amazon.com/Dash-Buttons/b?ie=UTF8&node=10667898011*

☒	Question	Why this matters
☐	6.1.10 When selling outcomes, do your customers see cost or improved services as more important?	If you are providing an outcome you need to define the strategy for that outcome such as customer value, lower cost, higher quality or quicker response. You might not have asked this question if you were providing a product to the customer where the question was one of quality vs. cost. In other words, your position in the market may change if you move from selling products and services to outcomes.
☐	6.1.11 Will your customer become the product?	IoT will facilitate the monetization of data streams which may generate more value than the product or service being sold. In the end, information about the customer becomes the product.
☐	6.1.12 How will selling outcomes impact your business risk?	Selling outcomes changes the relationship with customers. It is likely that you will have a deeper engaged with the customer which can reduce risk. However, you will also have a greater responsibility for delivering the promised business outcomes.
☐	6.1.13 Will your target market expand geographically?	IoT facilitates remote monitoring and service which can reduce services costs and may mean that it becomes economical to expand your target markets geographically.
☐	6.1.14 Will your product offering expand to include previously unprofitable products and services?	With the advent of the internet previously unprofitable low volume products and services became profitable to sell because of the reduction in marginal costs of distribution. With the advent of IoT and increased process automation and therefore reduced process costs this may lead to a larger breadth of products and services being sold.

6.2 Business model change

There has been much talk about "new business models" since the advent of the internet. Indeed, some academics[63] have demonstrated a relationship between the use of the term business model and the number NASDAQ listed technology stocks since the advent of the internet. What is clear then is that new technologies lead to new business models.

The exact definition of what is a business model and its components can vary depending on whom you ask. But accepting that at a high level a business model is intended to describe "how" a business achieves its stated strategy then one can ask a number of questions to decipher what will make up "how" they go about their business in the IoT.

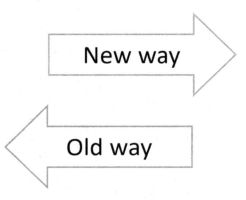

[63] Osterwalcer, A., Pigneur, Y., & Tucci, C. L. (2005). Clarifying business models: Origins, present, and future of the concept. *Communications of the association for Information Systems, 16*(1), 1

☒	Question	Why this matters
☐	6.2.1 What key activities will you need to undertake to enable your business model under IoT?	These are the most import activities in executing your businesses value proposition. If your value proposition changes under IoT then these activities must change as well. With so much potential for change it will be critical for you to have clarity about the key business activities required to enable that change. From finance to sales, manufacturing to customer support all areas of your business could be impacted.
☐	6.2.2 What are the key resources necessary to create value for your customers with IoT?	This is the human, financial, physical and intellectual property resources that your business will need to execute its new business model under IoT. Do these change and are they given the right priority in terms of your new business model?
☐	6.2.3 How will your partner network change with IoT?	As mentioned a few times in this book, IoT based solutions and outcomes will likely be delivered by consortiums of solutions providers, each providing one link in the chain. Have you assessed the impact of this on your current partnerships and whether you need to start fostering new ones?
☐	6.2.4 Will increased customer intimacy require new business processes?	As IoT allows vendors to connect directly to customers and understand them better, it also means that vendors will need to change their business processes to support more customer interaction. For example, when Microsoft moved from selling Office to selling Office 365 on line they had to greatly expand their call centers and customer service capabilities to support the increased level of direct customer interaction these new business models would bring.

☒	Question	Why this matters
☐	6.2.5 What is the value proposition in our new business model?	Value creation and value capture may change in your new IoT Business Model. In IoT the majority of the value is rarely in the actual thing or sensor, rather it is in the data, solution and outcome that is provided. The value proposition for your business may change with IoT.
☐	6.2.6 If your customers change does that mean that your sales and services organization changes?	As previously mentioned, IoT brings end customers closer to vendors. The supply chain becomes disintermediated and the level of customer intimacy goes up. This implies additional workload on the vendor as their direct customers will change from being the distributers and retailers to the end customer and they have to handle a higher volume of interactions.
☐	6.2.7 Does your target customer segments change? Should you be segmenting out customers differently?	Supply chain disintermediation and increased customer intimacy also means that you may have to segment these new customers differently as their potential value to you may change, requiring different service models.
☐	6.2.8 What technologies will your IoT solutions be based on?	Different technologies will likely drive different business models depending on the level of integration they provide.

☒	Question	Why this matters
☐	6.2.9 Will your finances (Cost Structures and Revenue Streams) be impacted by IoT?	Under IoT, certain revenue streams my dry up and others will be created. What is clear is that the trend towards outcomes and as-a-Service models means that profits go down in the short term as the revenue is spread out. However. longer term this will be better for the company as it means enhanced revenue predictability. In the short term, the company will need to make sure it has the cash flow to sustain this business model shift.
☐	6.2.10 Does the increased responsiveness that real time telemetry of the product provides represent a differentiator for your customers?	Technology may increase the speed at which you get information from your customers. But unless your business processes adapt to take advantage of that speed your customers may end up becoming disappointed rather than excited. For example, an elevator manufacturer that provides real time telemetry indicating that an elevator is in imminent risk of failure may only frustrate customers when they tell them that they don't provide 24/7 support and the elevator breaks down before this increased level of information can be taken advantage of.
☐	6.2.11 Can increased information about your customers' usage patterns allow you to understand them better and provide more tailored service offerings?	IoT can provide greater insights into your customers. Using this data to better understand them may enable you to offer more tailored service offerings through different business models. This can increase customer satisfaction and hence customer loyalty.

☒	Question	Why this matters
☐	6.2.12 Do you have an IoT specific security strategy?	There will be increased spending on IT security to defend against new IoT based threats increases. IoT provides numerous new attack vectors that haven't been accounted for in classical IT security and increases the threats to physical security. Business processes may need to be adapted to address these increase security implications.
☐	6.2.13 Does your product or solution use software that would benefit from regular updates with new features and functions?	New software based features and capabilities can be deployed to the field automatically. This means that product life cycles will increase but that product lock in increases as customers purchase new hardware less frequently.
☐	6.2.14 With increased information can your processes be more automated?	IoT facilitates more process automation and therefore less people resources.
☐	6.2.15 Will your IT strategy need to address the new volumes of information that IoT generates?	IoT is one of the biggest drivers of Big Data analysis in businesses these days. If you start to connect large volumes and varieties of devices to the internet to collect data you need to make sure you have some place to store the data and effective tools and methods to analyze and act on the data. Remember that most of the value from IoT doesn't come from connecting the device to the internet but from doing something proactive with the data is does generate.

X	Question	Why this matters
☐	6.2.16 Is speed of response key to your business success and represent a differentiator?	IoT enables improved time to respond by eliminating steps in the supply chain or services processes.

6.3 Operations, process and people changes

Underpinning the business strategy and business model are the resources required to achieve that strategy and model. After validating "what" your business strategy is and "how" you would achieve that business strategy through your business model one then needs to tie this back to changes in resource requirements. Resources can take many forms from the people that support your organization, to the physical assets such as office buildings, warehouses and factories required to the technology and IT resources needed to support it. Business processes and organizational design may also need to be considered. The view here is that whilst IoT will no doubt generate some operational efficiencies and reduction in the resources required, the bigger impact will be in the redistribution and reprioritization of

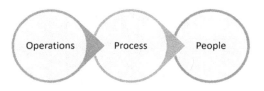

these resources as business strategy and models change.

☒	Question	Why this matters
☐	6.3.1 Do you believe there is opportunity to improve manufacturing efficiencies?	IoT enables improved monitoring of production facilities by enabling integration across multiple facilities and improved insights.
☐	6.3.2 Is labor a significant cost to your company?	IoT provides the ability to track your employee activity in detail (e.g. NFC Employee ID Cards).
☐	6.3.3 Do you have significant remote assets?	IoT provides the ability to reduce the labor costs required to support these assets. For example, farmers who have wells scattered across their property that need to be kept functioning to water livestock. Instead of paying full time hired hands to wonder around and periodically check those wells, they attach small IoT sensors that identify when then wells run dry or have collapsed. This means acreages can be managed by fewer hired hands who spend more of their time on actual maintenance than inspection.
☐	6.3.4 Does the majority of your workforce work remotely?	IoT provides the ability to track your employee activity in detail (e.g. GPS connected trucks). Activities that impact employee efficiency (and job satisfaction) can be identified and dealt with. For example, are employees taking the optimal route from job to job? Are they coming back to the office frequently for supplies and to complete other tasks which could be eliminated?

☒	Question	Why this matters
☐	6.3.5 Will supply chain disintermediation and increased customer intimacy mean more resources to manage your customers?	IoT facilitates direct contact between vendors and end customers often eliminating distributors, retailers and other partners as intermediaries. This direct route to your customer can facilitate more customer intimacy but it can also mean that you will need more resources to manage that increased level of customer contacts.
☐	6.3.6 Will providing outcomes as opposed to products and services mean a shift from manufacturing and inventory management to more service resources?	Investment is manufacturing and distribution may shift to investments in services and support as product life cycles extend requiring less product to be shipped but customers expecting an outcome require more interaction from their vendors.
☐	6.3.7 Will your incentives to your sales staff need to change?	Perhaps one of the bigger changes that happened in the IT industry when there was a move to as-a-Service models was that the incentives for the sales and technical staff had to change. Instead of them getting bonused on selling the big deal up front their bonus structure had to change to incentivize them based on customer success which ultimately lead to more revenue.

☒	Question	Why this matters
☐	6.3.8 Will the structure of your sales organization need to change?	The move to as-a-Service models has meant a general shift from business development in sales to account management. The focus of the sales forces changes from selling one offs to ongoing customer management. This means a change in the structure and skill sets of your sales work force.
☐	6.3.9 Does your manufacturing or the products you sell require regular maintenance?	Rather than having a services technician spend time inspecting and monitoring equipment to identify problems, IoT can automate this process and establish proactive maintenance activities. This can increase the efficiency of your operations and enhance customer satisfaction.
☐	6.3.10 Is post-sales support a significant cost for your customers? Will more accurate telemetry enable more efficient use of support resources?	IoT has the potential, through greater real-time insights to reduce the time post-sales support staff spend reactively identifying problems and redirects their efforts to proactively addressing issues. This can increase customer satisfaction and reduce reputational risks.

6.4 External stakeholders

As company Directors, a key role is to
ensure your company's external
stakeholders are being well served.
Whether this is your shareholders, your
customers, the companies who help
finance you, or the industry and
government agencies which hold you
accountable to uphold the law, they all
have a vested interest.

IoT has the potential to disruptively change business strategy,
business models and revenue streams. Also, the ability for IoT to
increase the connections between the physical and virtual worlds
introduces new and expanded business and security exposures.
These could increase risks and liability to the business, however, if
managed well then risks could be reduced due to greater insights
and speed of response.

Ensuring shareholders and other external stakeholders are kept
informed about these changes to revenue streams, short term
profitability and business risks and liability will be critical. Those
businesses that handle communications well in this area, will
differentiate themselves in the market.

An example - In April 2012 Abobe Systems made an "all in" shift
to subscription licensing through their Creative Cloud offering.
There were concerns in the IT industry about how customers and
shareholders would react[64]. However, through clear and positive
communications they managed their external stakeholder's
expectations and their share price responded very positively.

Adobe (NASDAQ: ADBE)

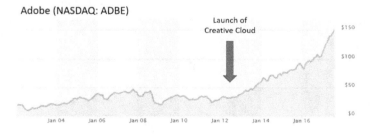

---

[64] *http://www.digitalartsonline.co.uk/news/creative-software/analysis-real-reason-adobe-ditched-creative-suite-for-creative-cloud/*

☒	Question	Why this matters
☐	6.4.1 How will Director liability change due to the increase of security issues?	In recent IoT attacks, hackers used coopted IoT devices to launch attacks against other third parties. There is talk of legislation to make companies responsible if the IoT devices they own are used to launch attacks against other third parties. Do you need to consider cyber insurance?
☐	6.4.2 How will Director liability change due to privacy issues?	New privacy legislation increases the responsibility of companies regarding the private data they collect from their customers. The increase in data collected about customers using IoT may increase the liability for company directors. However, addressing these issues could create a positive differentiator for you within your customer base.
☐	6.4.3 Will customers have concerns regarding the data you collect about them?	When asked most people want increased levels of privacy even though they themselves will take little action to ensure their own privacy. This is called the Privacy Paradox. Your customers may start questioning you about your products and services because of the data you are capturing about them through IoT. Being clear about how you use the data and how you meet or exceed compliance rules will be key. Equally showing how you use the data to provide benefits for the customer will help them see benefits not just risks.

☒	Question	Why this matters
☐	6.4.4 Will your distribution partners have concerns about the data you are collecting from end customers?	Some distribution partners may become concerned about the data you are collected about their end customers. IoT has the ability to disintermediate supply chains. Your distribution partners may be concerned that you are going to put them out of business. Proactive discussions with partners will aid in the transition.
☐	6.4.5 How does liability change due to the increased number of connections to the internet?	In a recent Denial of Service attack, simple consumer devices connected to the internet were coopted to launch a large internet attack on commercial web sites. The consumers who owned these devices largely did not know that their devices had been coopted. There is the possibility that equipment your company owns, connected to the internet could be coopted to launch an attack on a third party. A clear risk assessment and appropriate mitigation strategies can enhance your reputation for good governance and outweigh any potential for increased liability.
☐	6.4.6 How will your shareholders be impacted by profitability changes arising from new IoT business models?	IoT has the ability to enable new as-a-Service models. These new as-a-Service models can cause a decrease in profitability in the short term even though they will increase business valuation in the longer term. Communication of these changes will need to be handled proactively with shareholders highlighting the longer-term benefits.

☒	Question	Why this matters
☐	6.4.7 Do you have a large unionized workforce?	Job changes due to IoT, including enhanced employee monitoring and possible workforce reductions using IoT, may become the cause of concern with your unions. Early communications will be key.
☐	6.4.8 Will government regulators impose new regulations that could impact your deployment of IoT?	Most government legislation and regulation is in its infancy in terms of recognizing the impacts of IoT. Yet governments state the IoT is a concern for them in terms of privacy. It is highly likely that future regulation could impact how and where you implement IoT technologies. Being engaged in the bodies that are shaping this emerging legislation could be a positive investment.
☐	6.4.9 How will the data these devices collect provide greater corporate visibility and how will this impact corporate liability?	Whilst greater visibility will no doubt reduce risk and could in one way protect you from legal action by allowing you to be more proactive, greater information on your operations provided through IoT could also be used against you. It will be important to have a strategy to maximize the benefits whilst minimizing the liabilities from this new level of information.

☒	Question	Why this matters
☐	6.4.10 How will a move to providing outcomes affect returns, business risk and risk to shareholders?	In the move to as-a-Service software models the IT industry ended up taking on the risk of ensuring uptime on the solutions they were providing, which included guarantees and associated penalty clauses in contracts. This meant that some risk and the responsibility for success was transferred from the customer to the vendor. Invariably the customer ended up paying more to the vendor for taking on this risk in the long run and there was increased customer lock-in. Both of these could be seen as benefits to the vendor. But there was also a potential downside that may create risk to shareholder returns which must be managed.

Chapter

Delivering IoT

Problems are not stop signs, they are guidelines

Robert H. Schuller (Christian evangelist, 1926 – 2015)

Y OU are motivated, the organization is ready to follow you and you are clear about the business changes that are coming. So now we need to think about the delivery of IoT.

Whilst this section is about technology IT IS NOT TECHIE so please read on. We are NOT diving deep, we ARE looking at the areas that you need awareness of so you can shape the conversation. These questions could be used as the checklist to ensure the delivery teams have covered the business bases and not got lost in the technology weeds.

The questions in this section are based around the big themes shown in the diagram.

- Things capture data, which is transferred over networks, then stored and processed to deliver insights and actions.

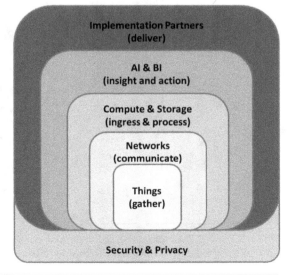

- To deliver this you will need to work with external parties. However, this is not a mature market and whilst a growing number of vendors, systems integrators and consultancies have entered the IoT market over the past few years, they are not all born equal.
- The explosion of data that is captured from everywhere and about everything will raise questions about security. The use of this data to generate new insights will also raise issues about privacy.

There are three primary challenges with delivering IoT[65]:

1. The diversity of the technologies available and the lack of widely adopted standards means that the choices are almost unlimited.
2. The immaturity of the technologies means there are adoption risks.
3. Any IoT solution will be delivered by an ecosystem of partners which means potentially managing a large number of partners to execute a solution.

In this chapter, we ask the questions that will help shape your thinking across these areas.

---

[65] Westerlund, M., Leminen, S., & Rajahonka, M. (2014). Designing business models for the internet of things. Technology Innovation Management Review, 4(7), 5

7.1 Implementation partners

This section is focused on the implementation partners and not the vendor or technology partners (we get to them in the Infrastructure section next). This is an immature market so selecting and then monitoring the performance of your partners will be critical to success.

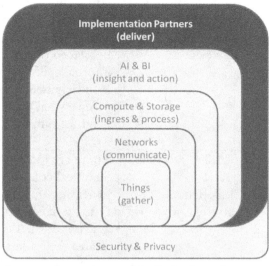

Balancing the risks of an innovative startup with limited track record against a larger, more financially stable but less nimble organization needs to be carefully considered.

With the hype surrounding IoT many organizations, both large and small, are trying to establish themselves in this market. It is important to scratch below the surface veneer of marketing to establish the actual credibility, capability and compatibility with your business.

☒	Question	Why this matters
☐	7.1.1 What role do you want your internal resources to have?	It is important to be clear about the role you want to play (from supervisory to detailed involvement in delivery). This creates clarity of the expectations that will be placed on the external partners and the internal skills required. You may need to review whether the business has the right skills, whether you need to train existing staff and/or hire new.
☐	7.1.2 Do you need independent strategy support?	There are lots of companies offering technical solutions and services. But who is providing the business oversight for you? Do you need an unbiased external party to assist with the business and/or technology strategy? Understanding the core focus of the partner will allow you to use them in the most appropriate manner.
☐	7.1.3 Do you need a custom or a commodity service?	"Uniqueness" will add cost (potentially significant), so it is important to assess if you can gain sufficient value add to justify a customized vs a standardized offering? Check how much of your business needs can be met with configuration rather than customization.
☐	7.1.4 Who is the prime partner, is there a single "throat to choke"?	The complexities of IoT will probably mean multiple parties will be involved. To avoid confusion in roles and responsibilities it is typical to have a primary point of management. This may be the role that your internal teams play, or it may be that you appoint a prime contractor. Project management skills will be critical.

☒	Question	Why this matters
☐	7.1.5 What are your timescales?	Shorter timescales increase the resources required and typically increase risk. A phased approach may increase time to total benefit capture, but it will allow a focus on benefit capture as soon as possible.
☐	7.1.6 What is the geographic reach of your project?	If you are deploying on a multinational scale then you will need a partner who either has direct resources in each location, or a prime contractor who can work with local resources. If you are deploying to a single or small number of locations in a localized area then a local supplier may be sufficient and offer other benefits such as local knowledge.
☐	7.1.7 Are you strongly aligned to your existing infrastructure suppliers and partners?	If you have made significant investments in a specific supplier for your current systems (e.g. GE, Microsoft, Salesforce) then it may be optimal to work with partners who specialize in this area.
☐	7.1.8 Do you need specific certifications from your supply partners?	Your commercial relationships with your customers may require you to show compliance both within your own business and with your supply chain. Do your partners need to meet ISO standards, or do their staff need specific security clearance? As far as specific IoT certifications, these are not yet mature and tend to be technically focused. You may need to work with multiple local standards.
☐	7.1.9 What is the partner's industry vertical experience?	Working with partners who have deep knowledge of your industry or business processes can give value to the project and provide closer alignment to your business outcomes.

☒	Question	Why this matters
☐	7.1.10 How central is IoT to the partner's service offering?	IoT is hot, so people want to be involved, but not all have real world experience. Partners with a clear and stable IoT strategy, who have been early adopters and have scars to prove it may be a better bet than those who are new to the party.
☐	7.1.11 What is the partners IoT experience?	In innovative spaces, it can be difficult to find partners with extended experience. Make sure you have scratched beneath the marketing veneer.
☐	7.1.12 Who are the partner's reference customers?	Check these not just for proof of competence, but also for potential support from other early adopters. Even when people see competitive advantage, they may be willing to share their experiences.
☐	7.1.13 What is "plan B" if the partner goes under?	In emerging markets, you may need to use smaller partners to get the skills required. However, they may not have a long term financial record or strong backers. This should not stop you using them but having a "plan B" should be part of your risk management approach.
☐	7.1.14 What role do you want the partner to provide for support services?	Deployment of IoT can result in significant increases in support calls as the data captured by the devices can create automated fault or alert requests. You should check if your existing in-house support systems can manage these volumes or if will you need your partners to provide this (especially 1st line triage)

☒	Question	Why this matters
☐	7.1.15 What relationships does the partner have with other delivery partners?	If multiple partners are required it can be very helpful if they have established working relationships. Whether this be commercial (vendor/reseller) or a practical shared delivery experience.
☐	7.1.16 Is the partner active in industry and user IoT groups?	Partners who are active in external bodies are showing that they have experience to share and a willingness to learn from their peers. In an emerging market, this can set them apart and help reduce risk for you.
☐	7.1.17 If you are benefiting from a delivery partners intellectual property (IP), what rights do you have on an ongoing basis?	In mature markets, basic processes are well known and available from many providers. However, in immature markets this knowledge maybe considered IP. Working with a partner who has these skills will assist your project. But what are your rights to use this over time, especially if the partner goes out of business.
☐	7.1.18 What "non-cash" value does your adoption of IoT offer to your delivery partners?	A successful project and a happy customer can be valuable asset for the partners marketing efforts. Offering to participate in a case study may create goodwill that can assist during times of project stress.

7.2 Infrastructure

As discussed this is an emerging and still complex space. Large scale technology vendors such as Microsoft (Azure) and Amazon (AWS) are offering generic platforms. Industrial giants such as GE (Predix[66]) and Hitachi (Lumada[67]) are aligning integrated IoT around their existing offerings. There are specialists in industry verticals such as

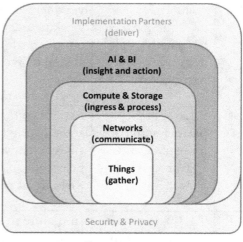

dairy farming[68] and Vineyard management[69]. Companies such as Salesforce[70] and ServiceNow with strong rules based process engines are positioning as platforms to drive business actions.

There are also hundreds of organizations, established and startup, who offer technology solutions at each level of the IoT stack. Some specialize in the Things[71], whilst others focus on the networks[72]. Global public cloud players and local service providers are providing compute and storage infrastructure. To ensure the data that is collected does not remain unused[73] there are multiple businesses who are focusing on the intelligence side of things.

Bringing these together will be complex, however, no matter how much some people get excited about the technology itself, we must always remember that it is just a tool to assist in delivering a business outcome. So, in this section our aim is to help you think about the technology themes rather than the technology itself.

---

[66] https://www.ge.com/digital/predix

[67] https://www.hitachiinsightgroup.com/en-us/lumada.html

[68] http://www.scrdairy.com/

[69] https://www.ericsson.com/assets/local/news/2015/10/iot-connected-vineyards.pdf

[70] https://www.salesforce.com/products/salesforce-iot/overview/

[71] https://urbanise.com/platform/iot-sensors/

[72] https://www.thinxtra.com/ and https://www.sigfox.com/

[73] http://www.engineering.com/IOT/ArticleID/11759/IBM-Watson-IoT-Platform-to-Help-Engineers-with-Product-Development.aspx

☒	Question	Why this matters
☐	7.2.1 What sort of IoT platform do you need?	From deployment and management of devices through to the visualization of insights and automated actions, the range of services required to deliver an IoT environment is complex. Even if you are starting small it is unlikely that you will want to build these services yourself. There are many platforms available and understanding your business strategy and organizational readiness will guide you. • Some platforms such as Microsoft Azure, Amazon AWS and IBM Watson offer a building blocks approach. Their ecosystem of partners will use these blocks to build out industry vertical solutions. • Others such as GE and Hitachi have created tightly integrated solutions around their existing industrial offerings. • Companies with strong business rules engines such as Salesforce and ServiceNow can drive business actions • There are solutions aligned to specific industry verticals • Startups offering independent end-to-end solutions are growing rapidly.
☐	7.2.2 Have you carried out an audit of your current systems environment and infrastructure?	Companies typically have multiple systems within their business and significant existing infrastructure. You may already have IoT devices deployed, can they be integrated or will they need to be replaced? Do existing systems need to co-exist and if so how easy will this be? Your existing systems may give you a head start OR they may be a blocker. It is better to invest the time early on, rather than find out later.

☒	Question	Why this matters
☐	7.2.3 Have you done a systems risk analysis from a business perspective?	Having a detailed understanding of the risks from a business perspective (likelihood and impact) associated with a loss of service, data etc. will assist in implementing appropriate mitigation strategies within your IoT infrastructure.
☐	7.2.4 Who understands the licensing terms of the various suppliers?	Licensing can be complex with different pricing models based on various measures e.g. users, devices, data ingress/egress, storage, processing and actions. These variations can have a fundamental impact on the economics of your project. Having a detailed understanding of licensing can help shape the way you select and deploy the services from the outset, rather than getting a shock later.
☐	7.2.5 Does a current primary systems supplier have a strong IoT offering?	An increasing number of suppliers are enhancing their existing offerings to incorporate IoT. Think carefully about whether these enhanced services are sufficient to meet your needs. It may be that starting from scratch could offer a better solution, however this needs to be offset against potential change risks.
☐	7.2.6 How much growth do you need to build into your infrastructure?	If the predictions/hype are true then we will be deploying an exponentially growing number of devices. Thinking about how big this will get for you and whether everything in your infrastructure can scale both locally and globally, will help future proof your investments.

☒	Question	Why this matters
☐	7.2.7 Are you using IoT to support real time operations?	The degree of infrastructure resilience required for real time industrial systems (power station) is significantly different to non-time critical or long-term data gathering (fencing on a farm, weather station). The same point is made below with respect to security.
☐	7.2.8 How do you ensure Data Trust?	Believing the accuracy of the data that is captured, transmitted and stored is essential and will increase based on the criticality of the data. You may need multiple devices collecting the "same" data or other validation metrics to increase confidence.
☐	7.2.9 How do you ensure Processing Trust?	Having confidence in the outcomes of analysis and your ability to come to the correct conclusions is necessary before you can carry out actions. Determining the appropriate checks and balances will depend on the nature of your operating environment. In mission-critical environments this may require multiple separate systems that must agree on a result before action is taken.
☐	7.2.10 Do you have a strategy for digital twins[74]?	Capturing data about the physical world allows this to be represented within the virtual. This allows monitoring, "what if" analysis. However, this needs a more sophisticated platform.

---

[74] http://www.gartner.com/newsroom/id/3482617

☒	Question	Why this matters
☐	7.2.11 How leading edge do you want to be in visualizing your data?	A digital twin model opens the opportunity for augmented reality. Engineers could "walk around" a piece of equipment and visualize its operating status without having to be physically present. Imagine watching the inside of an aero engine on a plane that is in flight. These ideas may have huge business benefits, but you will be on the leading/bleeding edge.
☐	7.2.12 Where is the focus of your SLA's and what level do you require?	Just because you can ask for 99.999% does not mean you need it. Higher service levels typically create rapid cost increases. Being clear about the critical points in your business process will ensure that you apply the right service levels in the right place. Does the Pareto principle apply[75]?
☐	7.2.13 Does your environment have variable workloads?	Environments often operate with peaks and troughs. This may be intraday (the 9am morning rush) or it could be specific a time of the month/year. There can also be unpredictable bursts. Ideally your infrastructure should be able to scale to these peaks, without having to pay for the capacity all the time (like the Cloud "as-a-Service" model)
☐	7.2.14 What are your business continuity and disaster recovery (BC/DR) requirements?	Things break. The nature and criticality of your environment will determine the level of BC/DR investments. Be clear about how often you should carry out recovery rehearsals, how much data can you afford to lose (RPO – recovery point objective) and how quickly you need to recover (RTO – recovery time objective).

---

[75] *https://en.wikipedia.org/wiki/Pareto_principle*

☒	Question	Why this matters
☐	7.2.15 What are your step-in rights?	It is likely that large parts of your infrastructure will be provided by third parties e.g. cloud service providers, communications network providers. It is also possible that due to market immaturity, one of these suppliers could go out of business. If this happens you should consider if you need a Plan B and whether you or a prime contractor need step in rights to allow the systems to keep operating.
☐	7.2.16 What is the legal jurisdiction for supplier contracts?	Your suppliers may be located overseas and have contracts that are based on jurisdictions outside of your operating country. How important is this to you? Do you have access to legal experience in these locations if required?
☐	7.2.17 Do your roll out plans require parallel running?	You may wish to parallel run prior to switch over to gain confidence (data and processing trust). Consider if there are better times of the year for this happen and whether this helps set project timelines?
☐	7.2.18 What are the deployment constraints for the IoT devices?	There may be specific constraints such as size, operating temperature etc. The ease of access to a sensors location will determine factors such as resilience, durability and battery life. In remote or adverse operating environments, it may be cost effective to install multiple devices to allow for failures.

☒	Question	Why this matters
☐	7.2.19 Do devices need power supplies or can they be battery powered?	Providing power to where an IoT device is deployed can create cost barriers (approvals, electricians, cabling etc.). Battery powered IoT devices are more convenient to deploy, but bring compromises such as minimizing the time they are active.
☐	7.2.20 Are the different parts of your IoT infrastructure designed/certified to work together?	The lack of established and well adopted standards means this cannot be taken for granted. An integrated solution from a single supplier may offer some comfort, but could result in compromises in other areas such as functional fit for your desired business outcomes.
☐	7.2.21 How sophisticated do the devices need to be?	To gain device ubiquity there has been a focus on reducing cost and hence simplification of the devices capability. However, depending on your business needs you may need greater sophistication and this can limit your choices and increase your costs, both financially and with respect to device management. Data volumes, network reliability, localized processing, security requirements may all affect the requirement for localized storage and compute at the device.
☐	7.2.22 What needs to be sensed?	The relatively low cost of IoT devices compared to the deployment costs may make it cost effective to deploy sensors to capture multiple conditions. This could allow you capture both the specific data you need today as well as data points you could potentially use in the future.

☒	Question	Why this matters
☐	7.2.23 How frequently do you need to capture data to meet the business need?	Capturing data has a cost in power at the device. Where IoT devices are battery powered the amount of "Sleep time" will impact their lifespan. For higher frequencies, you may also need local storage (with associated challenges) to overcome any network reliability issues.
☐	7.2.24 Do you need to capture high volume data such as video or will a simple binary (on/off, open/closed) be sufficient?	Data volumes have a basic impact on network design. Long range, low bandwidth, low power networks such as SigFox and LoRa have a very different price point to high bandwidth solutions such as 4G mobile networks. For example, do you may need a video camera (high volume) to check if a door is open or would a simple open/closed (few bytes) sensor be sufficient.
☐	7.2.25 What volume of data is going to be transmitted?	Larger volumes require faster, higher cost networks. There is also the issue of scalability so that your network can keep up with your growth. Whilst an individual devices data transfer may not be large, when you consider the total number of devices it could grow significantly.
☐	7.2.26 How much data can you lose?	Devices fail, networks have reliability issues. You need to understand what level of data loss is acceptable. Monitoring fences on a farm will have a different answer to an oil refinery.
☐	7.2.27 Do you need a local, national or global network infrastructure?	A local network may be sufficient for a single warehouse, however if monitoring a shipping container then integrated global coverage may be required.

☒	Question	Why this matters
☐	7.2.28 How and where is security applied in the data transmission process?	Different providers implement transmission security in different ways. Being clear about what is provided by the infrastructure and where you have responsibility will be critical to ensuring security is maintained.
☐	7.2.29 Can your storage solution scale to our needs over time?	Storage is relatively low cost, but it is not free. Volumes can increase rapidly as you add more devices and increase the retention period. You should have a plan for how you scale your storage solution over time and what the pricing model is?
☐	7.2.30 How time-critical is the processing of captured data?	The requirements for the time taken from data capture to analysis and actions will vary wildly depending on your business needs. The shorter the timeframe the higher the costs. Getting the balance right will optimize performance against cost.
☐	7.2.31 What timeframe of data do you need for active decision making?	If you are monitoring whether a door is open you only need the latest data to trigger actions. However, you may wish to keep historical data for long term analysis. Determining what data is dynamic and what is static can impact your approach to storage and significantly impact costs.
☐	7.2.32 Who owns the data that is captured?	If you are capturing data about 3rd parties (e.g. FitBit) then your contracts should be clear about data ownership and usage rights as this can impact your ability to derive value from it.

☒	Question	Why this matters
☐	7.2.33 How do you access your data in the event of termination or exit?	With a lack of standards, you could find yourself locked in to a supplier. Check how easy it is for you to migrate to another service and whether your data can be provided to you in well-known formats that can simplify the process of importing into other systems.
☐	7.2.34 Do you have specific requirements for where data centers are located?	Part of the attraction for the "as-a-Service" model is that the details of operations are taken care of by someone else. However, you may have legal, contractual or moral obligations to use "in country" services. Also, don't forget to check where the supplier stores data for reliability and disaster recovery purposes.
☐	7.2.35 Do your customers require data segregation?	Some existing customer contracts may have clauses that require you to store their data separate from others. Alternatively, this could also be a value add that you can offer.
☐	7.2.36 Do you need to migrate data from existing systems to your IoT platform?	You may have data in existing systems that needs to be migrated to your IoT platform. This maybe a one-off process if the legacy systems are being replaced or ongoing if they are staying in operation.
☐	7.2.37 Do you need access to 3rd party data to provide the required insights?	Your business requirements may require external data to deliver the insights you require. Validating the commercial and technical terms for accessing this and how regularly the data needs to be updated may impact both costs and systems design.

☒	Question	Why this matters
☐	7.2.38 Will you be able to combine data from different sources to provide a single view?	The lack of standards may result in data being captured and stored in varying formats. You will need common "keys" that link different data sources together. Getting your data storage design right up front is important, however flexibility to adapt as you learn more and your requirements change is important as well. This is the area of Data Semantics[76].

7.3 Security and privacy

In 2015, the director of the NSA, Michael Rogers[77], outlined 3 things that keep him awake at night[78]

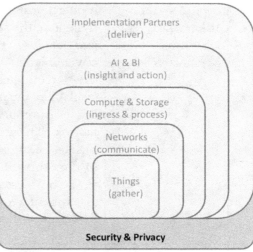

- **Cyber-attacks that do infrastructure damage** - "It is only a matter of 'when' that someone users cyber as a tool to do damage to the critical infrastructure of our nation."

- **Data manipulation** - "Historically, we've largely been focused on stopping the extraction of data and insights, but what happens when suddenly our data is manipulated and you no longer can believe what you're physically seeing?" he said.

- **Non-state actors** - "What happens when a non-state actor, who literally has no interest in the status quo - take ISIL for an example - starts viewing the web as not just a vehicle to generate revenue, to recruit, to spread the ideology, but instead they view it as a weapon system?"

Whilst these were about cyber threats in general, they are applicable to IoT as well. There is a general awakening to these concerns, however standards and guidance, whether it be from government bodies such as NIST[79], security vendors such as Trend Micro[80] or Industry bodies such as IoT Alliance Australia[81] are still emerging

> Security and privacy are not "set and forget". They need constant review and monitoring.

[77] https://en.wikipedia.org/wiki/Michael_S._Rogers
[78] https://www.businessinsider.com.au/nsa-chief-describes-3-biggest-cyber-threats-2015-10
[79] https://www.nist.gov/programs-projects/nist-cybersecurity-iot-program
[80] https://www.trendmicro.com/us/iot-security/
[81] http://www.iot.org.au/wp/wp-content/uploads/2016/12/IoTAA-Security-Guideline-V1.0.pdf

X	Question	Why this matters
☐	7.3.1 Have you done a systems risk analysis from a business perspective?	Technology is an indispensable part of the modern business. A risk assessment needs to include the security aspects of access and data loss. However, it also needs to cover areas such as the process logic and data integrity, end user acceptability, availability including people dependencies, as well as reputational, legal and ethical factors. These need to be viewed in a business context, considering the likelihood of the exposure occurring and the impact to the business if it did. This overall assessment allows mitigation strategies to be designed in a business context.
☐	7.3.2 Are you using IoT to support real time operations?	The business impact of an interruption in service when using IoT for real time operations (oil refinery, power station) is totally different to non-time critical or long-term data gathering (fencing on a farm, weather station). How you protect these should reflect this.
☐	7.3.3 Are you impacted by data security legislation both locally and overseas?	Governments around the world are legislating to protect citizens from the inappropriate use and retention of data. GDPR[82] impacts businesses holding data about European citizens, even if they are based outside of Europe. The Notifiable Data Breach[83] scheme requires Australian businesses to notify any individuals likely to be at risk of serious harm by a data breach.

---

[82] *http://www.eugdpr.org/*
[83] *https://www.oaic.gov.au/media-and-speeches/statements/mandatory-data-breach-notification*

☒	Question	Why this matters
☐	7.3.4 What is the position of your local company regulator to cyber threats?	Organizations charged with the oversight of corporate governance are making increasingly clear signs that they are monitoring businesses for their posture towards cyber threats. For example, ASIC in Australia state[84] "22. We will focus on serious breaches where these indicate: …(c) failure by corporations to respond appropriately to the threat of malicious cyber activity"
☐	7.3.5 Do you have an impact classification model for data that you collect and store?	Not all data is born equal. Some is designed to be in the public domain, some will have significant impact if shared. Not understanding this can lead to over or under engineering and poorly directed investment. Consideration should be given to the data in isolation, and the exposure when combined with other data. Other drivers will be legislation, reputational risks and social expectations.
☐	7.3.6 What is your liability if something goes wrong?	Questions about liability are asked in business all the time, however IoT expands the scope. Depending on your industry new exposures will emerge. For example: • Who is responsible if a driverless car has an accident – the driver or the manufacturer? • Who is responsible if a webcam is hacked and in turn is used to hack others? • What happens if a bad decision is made based on data from an IoT sensor?

---

[84] *http://asic.gov.au/about-asic/asic-investigations-and-enforcement/asic-enforcement-outcomes/*

☒	Question	Why this matters
☐	7.3.7 Is the exposure with individual data capture or the aggregation of data?	The data you gather may have limited exposure in isolation. However, when combined with other data greater exposures may occur.
☐	7.3.8 What are your rights to use the data you collect?	Your right to use the data that you collect needs to be clearly established. For "in-house" data this may be straight forward. But where it is external, especially where people are concerned, this may not be as straight forward. People are giving very personal health data to organizations like FitBit with little thought for the future use. You need to consider how you would be positioned both legally and ethically.
☐	7.3.9 Are you subject to data retention requirements?	You may be obligated legally, to retain data you capture for a certain period. Understanding what you do with the data at the end of any retention period and whether you need to have data discovery capabilities if access is requested will clarify any potential risks and liability.
☐	7.3.10 Do you have a segregation of responsibilities for monitoring and operating?	Despite best efforts, self-regulation often falls short of expectations. The pressures on operational activities to "get stuff done" means that "oversight" can take a poor back seat. New roles such as Chief Security Officer are intended to offer a separation between the operators and the people providing oversight. If nobody is watching AND taking actions then the best systems in the world cannot protect you - be clear about who is responsible for monitoring security.

☒	Question	Why this matters
☐	7.3.11 Who is responsible for considering new or emerging security threats?	IoT introduces new threats or simplifies existing ones e.g. physical theft, denial of sleep, incorporation into botnets, deliberate alteration of sensor data, signal jamming. These need to be considered in the context of: • Security Differentiators – the new threats unique to IoT • Security Multipliers – the enhancement of threats due to the volume of devices
☐	7.3.12 Does your data need to be encrypted?	The simple answer could be yes. However, be clear about where encryption occurs so you can minimize any exposure points in your infrastructure. If local to the device then more processing power and storage may be required (at extra cost). Also, if required, be clear about who maintains the encryption keys (a non-trivial task).
☐	7.3.13 Where in the overall infrastructure are security systems and processes located?	IoT infrastructure is complex and this complexity creates many entry points for security breaches. IoT devices are typically designed to be simple and low cost. Installing anti-malware may not be possible or will change the types of devices available. Transmission networks, data storage and AI systems all need to be considered and secured as appropriate.

☒	Question	Why this matters
☐	7.3.14 How do you manage trust between separate systems?	It is likely that your IoT infrastructure will want to share data across multiple systems. It is also likely that (due to the current lack of established standards) these separate systems will not have a common framework of trust. This will either mean sharing the data and "hoping" all is safe (what is your responsibility if it is not) or establishing an external trust framework. Your risk assessment will help in establishing the likelihood/business impact involved and hence the amount of effort required to mitigate the risks.
☐	7.3.15 What is the security posture of your suppliers?	Standards are still emerging so you are reliant upon the voluntary attitude of the supplier. Hopefully security is taken seriously and included within their offerings "by design".

Chapter

Funny you should say that

Laughter gives us distance. It allows us to step back from an event, deal with it and then move on.

Bob Newhart (Comedian, 1929 –)

IOT promises to bring changes that will significantly improve people's lives and the way we do business. The Smart Questions in this book will hopefully help you get started on your IoT journey. What the book is missing so far are some stories or anecdotes which bring these Smart Questions to life.

If we'd interspersed these stories with the questions it would have made the last Chapters too long. It would also have prevented you using the questions as checklists or aide-memoires. So, we've grouped together our list of stories in this Chapter. I'm sure that you have your own stories – both positive and negative - so let us know them:

stories@smart-questions.com

Commonwealth Bank, Wells Fargo and Brighann Cotton pioneer landmark blockchain trade transaction

"We strive to stay at the forefront of emerging technologies to enable greater efficiencies and solve the real world challenges our customers face. The interplay between blockchain, smart contracts and the Internet of Things could deliver considerable benefits throughout the global supply chain."

Dilan Rajasingham, Head of Emerging Tech, CommBank

 Challenge – the drivers to migrate

Trade finance is undeniably overdue for a technological makeover. Trade finance is a paper-based and labour-intensive exercise that relies heavily on the use of Letters of Credit (LoC). The process is inefficient and cumbersome.

It takes days, even weeks, to physically move the documents advising the exporter that the importer has the necessary funds to pay for the goods. The importer undergoes a similar ordeal awaiting notification of the goods' arrival at their destination before authorising payment.

Use of paper documents means that there are delays to the notification of title transfer. Funds and insurance are therefore unduly tied up at both ends.

 What was done

CBA, Wells Fargo, and Brighann Cotton undertook the first interbank trade finance deal using blockchain technology (Skuchain Inc's bracket technology), the Internet of Things and a smart contract.

The transaction was executed automatically through a series of smart contacts, shared on a private distributed ledger. A GPS tracking device provided real time data on the movements of the cargo.

The shipment had 88 bales of cotton, worth US$35,000, which were transported aboard the 54,309 tonne vessel called the Blue

Whale. The ship left the port of Houston, America, and docked at Qingdao, China in early November 2016.

The interplay between blockchain, smart contracts and the Internet of Things is a significant development towards revolutionising trade transactions and delivering considerable benefits throughout the global supply chain.

 Business outcome and benefits

The experiment shows how emerging technologies could eliminate inefficiencies, lower costs and improve security.

Time: With blockchain, all documentation (except bills of lading) is electronic. Documents can't be lost and the provenance of each document is established. There's no expense to courier original and duplicate documentation around the world and the transfer of information is almost instant. Also, the smart contract allows the documents to be automatically approved. The metadata that describes underlying documents is automatically matched off by the system confirming that the documents align to the initial contract between the buyer and seller. The smart contract system then confirms that payment (deferred or otherwise) is ready to be made. This reduces risk and cost, while increasing speed.

Transparency: By using one system, the process becomes completely transparent to designated parties. All players can track the transaction's progress, so all parties could track that goods were loaded and unloaded on the ship, linking payment and risk to the actual physical flow of goods (historically, these were linked to the paper flow). The real time nature of the contract means payment can be immediate, insurance policies can be flexible and parties have complete visibility over their liabilities.

Security: Invoices can't be duplicated and it is impossible for unauthorised parties to submit documents. This protects importers, exporters and their banks from fraud. Also, although the process is open and transparent for the parties involved, data is restricted to the appropriate participants and the entire process is invisible to those who do not have permission to see the ledger.

Cooperative Intelligent Transport Initiative, Centre for Road Safety, Transport for NSW.

The Cooperative Intelligent Transport Initiative (CITI) is a testing facility for Cooperative Intelligent Transport Systems (CITS). Based in the Illawarra region, it is the largest CITS test facility in the Southern Hemisphere. CITS allows vehicles to  communicate with other vehicles and infrastructure, such as traffic signals, that are fitted with the same system. Drivers then receive alerts about upcoming hazards that could cause a crash.*

http://roadsafety.transport.nsw.gov.au/research/roadsafetytechnology/cits/citi/index.html

 ### Cooperative Intelligent Transport Systems – Australia's largest CITS project

The Cooperative Intelligent Transport Initiative or CITI project is the largest in Australia to use Cooperative Intelligent Transport Systems (CITS) and the only one in the world to focus on heavy vehicles.

CITS use technology to allow vehicles to communicate with other vehicles, traffic signals and roadside infrastructure. The systems are also known as vehicle-to-vehicle communications, or vehicle-to-infrastructure communications. CITS increase the quality and reliability of information available to drivers about their immediate environment, other vehicles and road users.

 ### Challenge – the drivers to migrate

This technology allows drivers to receive safety messages about upcoming hazards that could cause a crash. The messages come from technology attached to the vehicles and infrastructure like traffic lights. The technology can determine the speed, braking and location of a vehicle. When it detects a potential crash with another vehicle equipped with the same technology, it alerts the driver with an audiovisual alert on their CITS device inside the vehicle.

The CITS device also shows when a vehicle is approaching a red light and alerts the driver if they go over the speed limit while travelling down Mount Ousley Road.

 What was done

The initiative is being held in the Illawarra region. So far, the project has fitted 60 trucks, 11 buses and three traffic lights with the technology, and continues to expand.

More than 2 billion records have been collected for analysis. A roadside transmission station broadcasts speed limit information to heavy vehicles about the 40km/h truck and bus zone down the Mount Ousley descent.

The project holds a licence from the Australian Communications and Media Authority to broadcast on the 5.9GHz radio spectrum.

Drivers in participating vehicles see the following messages:

- Intersection collision warning
- Heavy braking ahead warning
- Traffic signal phase information
- Speed limit information.

 Business outcome and benefits

Cooperative Intelligent Transport Systems have the potential to make our roads safer and more efficient.

The Centre for Road Safety will collect and analyse all the data from CITI, with the potential for the technology to enable driverless vehicles of the future to talk to each other.

Building a new future: Transforming Australia's construction industry with digital technologies.

"ATF Vision has developed leading edge affordable surveillance technology, delivering a valuable service for customers and generating a significant new stream of business for ATF Services."

Robin Mysell, ATF Services CEO   *http://www.atfservices.com.au*

 ## The context

ATF Services, a leading provider of security and safety solutions for Australia's construction industry, has launched a pioneering, intelligent, multisensor, IoT alarm system using Microsoft Azure Service Fabric and Azure IoT Edge. The firm teamed up with software developer Two Bulls to create a platform that connects low-powered IoT devices to Azure and a mobile app. Easily installed virtually anywhere, the new platform puts sophisticated site surveillance within reach of everyone from private homeowners to large construction firms.

 ## The drivers of change

According to IBISworld, Australia's construction sector is a $349 billion a year business – but one increasingly being targeted by criminals.

Tool theft from construction sites and vehicles is a global problem which is on the rise. A recent study revealed that 39 per cent of residential builders were affected by theft or vandalism at their building sites. Of those, two thirds had experienced more than one incident.

While 61 per cent experienced the theft of raw materials, 46 per cent had experienced the loss of small hand-held tools. The cost of replacing tools or materials is only one part of the equation: without the gear to get the job done, customers' projects get delayed and builders risk fines for delayed completion.

To combat the problem, ATF Services, working closely with Microsoft and Melbourne based digital consultancy Two Bulls, has developed the Secure Track Sense Security Multi-Sensor S1000 – a world-first IoT security device that provides continuous internet-connected monitoring for up to 12 months on just 4 AA batteries.

What was done

The Secure Track Sense Security Multi-Sensor S1000 is controlled via a mobile app, which allows the device to be configured to the requirements of the environment. Site managers can download an app to access automatic alerts which are sent via app notification and/or email if devices detect any unexpected activity such as movement or sound.

The Security Multi-Sensor is backed by the ATF Cloud platform, which is hosted on Microsoft's Azure and is designed on top of Microsoft's Service Fabric for reliability and scalability to support millions of concurrently connected devices.

The Security Multi-Sensor is the first in a suite of IoT products by ATF designed to secure, track and monitor environments and equipment to help reduce the loss of assets, prevent vandalism and monitor productivity. The solution is being offered as a value-added service to ATF clients through its specially formed division ATF Vision.

 ## Business outcome and benefits

The innovative solution is one of the first regional deployments of Microsoft's Service Fabric, and features a pioneering IoT Gateway implementation. Two Bulls used Microsoft's IoT Gateway to create a custom-built field gateway to connect the camera's industrial-grade multi-sensors to Azure.

Nick Darvey, technical lead for Two Bulls, said that Microsoft's Service Fabric, its programming models and high-availability made it a natural fit for ATF's requirements "as we don't have the twenty years of research and PhDs necessary to build our own distributed system".

Brett Shoemaker, Cloud + Enterprise Business Group Leader at Microsoft Australia, said: "Microsoft Azure's reach and resilience, along with the rich IoT platform and tools underpins this highly innovative security solution that can now be sold internationally to tackle a real and growing problem. ATF Services identified a major challenge facing its clients and has developed an intelligent, scalable and resilient solution that will deliver solid returns on investment by ensuring construction sites are secured and projects meet crucial deadlines."

Funny you should say that

The K-Tracker Project

"Being able to know where they are at all times and receive notifications immediately when things go wrong... I don't know how we did without this."

Jo Loader, Research Scientist　　*http://www.trackkoalas.com.au*

 ## The Context

The K-Tracker is a system designed as a response to the increasing risks facing one of Australia's iconic native creatures, the koala. Koalas have recently been listed as a vulnerable species, and monitoring programs are considered an essential part of the effort to ensure their survival. Although wildlife telemetry is not new and there are many animal-tracking solutions on the market, none quite fit the bill for koalas.

 ## The Challenge

Dr Jon Hanger took the project to LX Design House to solve the issues they were having with tracking koalas. The requirements of the project were extremely challenging and often conflicting- super small/light but with long battery life were two requirements in particular that came into conflict. Animal welfare was obviously the constraint that was impossible to compromise on, and presented some unique challenges. For example, koalas tuck their chins into their chests to rest (unlike most animals), making it unfeasible to have bulky electronics under their chin or a wide collar.

 ## The K-Tracker Solution

The K-Tracker had to achieve a solution that provided for the welfare of the animals being tracked. The collars have proven to be a great success for the welfare of the animals. Two months after first deployment onto dozens of koalas, reports showed no evidence of rashes or injuries caused by the collars. This is an extremely positive result, as this is the first time Dr Hanger had deployed a new collar in the field without a single instance of injury in the first 2 months.

The K-Tracker functions on Desktop, Android or iOS Device as a hosted web application that allows field staff to track Koalas on a map close to real-time from anywhere in the world. Dual sensor activity logging with motion profile analysis capabilities, orientation analysis, high-G + free fall detection, and automatic low activity email report generation provides a highly detailed picture of the state of individual koalas delivered as regular reports.

 Outcome and benefits

The K-Tracker device has successfully provided accurate tracking data without negatively impacting koala welfare. In the first two years of the tracking program during the data-gathering phase, there were 244 deaths. Using that data, controls were implemented and in the following 12 months there were only 32. The value of the contributions of the koala management program and its data to scientific/academic endeavours cannot be overstated. The program has provided unprecedented insights into the biology and ecology of koalas, and a huge number of data was collected over the nearly four years of the program.

As far as we are aware there is no other comparable device that provides the functionality of the K-Tracker at its weight and battery life. The K-Tracker is a highly-awarded product and one that has provided significant visibility for LX Design House's capabilities. This project is a demonstration of the capability of well-designed IoT solutions to make a real difference in the world, providing the data that allows us to target solutions that can potentially save endangered species.

Intelligent IoT Lighting
Drives Key Customer Savings

"The lighting solution of the future will be an integral part of the Internet of Things. It will be connected, collect and communicate data, and be capable of intelligently managing itself to deliver optimal lighting levels and minimum energy consumption"

Sam Redmond, Head of Business Development & Strategy
Vivid Industrial

www.vividindustrial.com

 ## Situation – context

As ever-increasing energy prices impact business competitiveness and viability, the requirement to reduce energy consumption has become a critical aspect of organisational survivability.

Given lighting typically represents between 10%-60% of an organisations total energy cost, Vivid Industrial developed MATRIXX®, a unique Australian designed and manufactured intelligent, energy efficient, IoT lighting platform which uses advanced data and control to consistently generate benchmarked lighting energy savings in excess of 90% to currently installed systems and in excess of 70% compared to standard LED systems.

This efficiency is achieved through the intelligent nature of MATRIXX® system, which monitors over 3.3 million data points annually per light, and adjusts in real time to environmental and operational factors to maximise the amount of energy saved.

Linfox progressive approach to energy management saw MATRIXX® installed at Dulux's flagship distribution center at Marsden Park in NSW Australia to help reduce energy costs accross the site.

 ## Challenge – drivers to migrate

The Dulux distribution center provided specific challenges including a dense high racking facility which demanded an above average high level light requirement of 225lux, which was around 40% higher than lux levels at other warehouses. This made the design and delivery of both a quality lighting outcome and sustained deep energy savings complex. In addition, the system had to be able to deal with summer month average temperatures at roof level exceeding 50 degrees Celsius.

Resolution - what was done

Vivid Industrial engineered an optimised site specific solution based on its award winning MATRIXX® intelligent lighting platform. The solution successfully provided high quality and consistent lighting across the site, meeting the customers high light output requirements and utilised its intelligent IoT capability to optimise natural daylight and operational patterns to maximise energy efficiency.

MATRIXX® 'Plug and Play' architecture also minimised installation and maintenance costs while providing consistent, measurable and verifiable lighting savings for over 10yrs or more. The modular design also provided flexibility for system redesign to meet changing business needs.

Leveraging its inbuilt intelligence, MATRIXX® was able to deliver high quality lighting output, improving productivity, health and safety and ultimately revenue, by fusing environmental sensor and device operational data with algorithm control, to continuously adjust on site system behavior for maximum efficiency, exceeding customer expectations.

 Benefits - business outcome

Vivid Industrial delivered a system that had to contend with providing **40% more light** output than a standard warehouse, all while delivering an industry leading **74% energy efficiency** compared to a comparable **LED system**, by constantly analysing **3.3 million data points** per light annually.

"The intelligent part of the system takes it to another level"
Linfox Sustainability Manger, Bo Christensen

MATRIXX® validated, modular, intelligent, IoT Lighting platform is designed to deliver tangible energy savings for customers globally. It's always powered and homogeneously placed core IoT lighting infrastructure, will accommodate any other IoT capability, future proofing the platform and augmenting its capability beyond an efficient lighting platform for customers.

Delivering major water savings to large enterprises and councils across Australia and New Zealand.

"Our smart water meter systems can detect leaks almost as soon as they occur thanks to the Sigfox nationwide network for the Internet of Things & a solid cloud management platform. For example, Fairfield Council, is saving $4,500 a month as a result of early leak detection."

Guenter Hauber-Davidson, Managing Director

www.watergroup.com.au

Empowering Internet of Things

www.thinxtra.com

 ## Situation

WaterGroup is one of the leading players in the smart water meter market in Australia helping both public and private sector customers manage their water supplies. Despite good management, water leaks still occur and if they go undetected they can result in both environmental challenges and financial shocks.

 ## Challenge

Despite the consequences of undetected leaks, with potentially millions of litres of water being lost, the costs & high power requirement of connectivity, limited WaterGroups ability to cost effectively deliver mass deployment of sensors across water networks. For businesses, especially large water consumers, this was not a viable option as the cost of sensing leaks was higher that the risk of a high water bill.

Watergroup needed a network solution that would allow smart sensors to reliably and securely transmit data over long distances at previously unachievable price points.

Resolution

WaterGroup carried out 24 months R&D on Low Power Wide Area Network (LPWAN) services that would work with smart water devices.

As a result, "Sigfox technology became an obvious choice for use as part of our smart water metering solution," says Guenter Hauber-Davidson, Managing Director of WaterGroup.

"Our smart water meter systems are so innovative they can now detect leaks almost as soon as they occur"

WaterGroup have now entered into a 5 year partnership with Thinxtra who are empowering the Internet of Things in Asia Pacific by deploying Sigfox long range, low power consuming connectivity networks as well as building a full eco-system of partners providing IoT solutions.

 ## Benefits

Councils and businesses across Australia and New Zealand can now benefit not only from automated meter readings but also valuable additional information on water use that helps save water and money. For example, Fairfield Council, saved $4,500 a month as a result of early leak detection. Also, Australian National University (ANU), saved over $300,000 within six weeks of smart meter system being installed."

Centratech Systems

"Working with AWS has changed our business. It shines a light on new technology and ways of working that we may have eventually discovered on our own, but we would have been so far behind the competition that we would be struggling to keep up."

CentraTechSystems

Richard Freedman, Managing Director   *www.centratech.com.au*

 ## Situation – the context

Centratech Systems is an Australian provider of wireless monitoring and control systems used by local governments to manage water, pumping, and electricity applications. CTS's strength lies in its many years of field experience in Australia. Its products and services are helping councils across the nation better manage scarce national resources, primarily water and electricity.

Until recently there were few to no competitors for CTS's services, but more IT-oriented companies are now entering the market. The company was facing pressure to modernize the devices and systems it offered local councils. A recurring request was for a more convenient way for field technicians to monitor devices across a broad territory from their trucks, without physically visiting each device or having specialized equipment on hand.

 ## Challenge – the drivers to migrate

The onboarding process for its legacy devices was grueling, requiring a six-hour, one-on-one training session for every technician who would interact with the pumps, meters, sensors, and filters installed in their areas. Furthermore, these first-generation smart devices, designed to communicate with centralized systems at council offices, were often too expensive for small local councils. This restricted CTS's business partners to larger entities such as the City of Melbourne, and constrained it's time to market due to training demands. The company's ability to innovate and perfect the devices and systems customers need is key to its success and market proposition. The millions of messages being exchanged between devices and their corresponding control panels required extensive coding and management of servers, further limiting labor resources. CTS needed a way to remove the heavy lifting required to maintain an increasingly complex network of devices.

 ## What was done

CTS was an earlier adopter of AWS EC2 to provide access to their services via internet enabled devices such as smartphones and tablets. In 2016 with the support of AWS and PolarSeven (an AWS Partner Network advanced consulting partner) they started using the AWS IoT Platform. CTS were able to install new types of IoT-enabled monitoring devices for electricity and water management applications, which are smaller and lighter than their first-generation predecessors. These modernized smart devices do less in the field and more in the cloud environment, and are thus simpler to operate. They also require less physical maintenance and are easier to switch out if a fault occurs. What's more, there is no limit to the number of users who can concurrently access the system, a requirement which the legacy device systems struggled with.

 ## Business outcome and benefits

CTS technicians now spend far less time driving around visiting physical devices, and can service more devices remotely from their IoT-enabled smartphones. The team is 50 percent more productive than it was just two years ago. "This is a huge bonus to a small business like ours, especially in Australia, where wages are high by world standards," says Freedman.

Shifting to the IoT server-less environment, the new smart devices which are approximately 66% less expensive than their predecessors and a reduction in training time from six hours to one, has triggered a critical change in CTS's cost structure. This has allowed CTS to approach smaller councils and agricultural customers, who were previously hesitant to consider CTS's services due to time and budget constraints.

Enhanced security features in the IoT environment have also been a major selling point in discussions with new clients. The extra encryption and mutual authentication associated with each connected IoT device gives CTS's public-sector customers confidence in the solutions they purchase. Security is particularly important to the local councils, as the monitoring and control systems access aspects of city and state infrastructure that could be vulnerable to outside threats. The Australian government also strictly oversees local agencies to ensure proper security protocols are in place.

AWS IoT is a managed service, which means CTS can focus on innovation instead of managing servers or infrastructure. Less than a year ago, the company released Field Mouse, its future flagship product. When it first launched, Field Mouse's purpose was to allow multiple users to concurrently control field lighting systems. It has since been expanded to water-management applications and operation of security gates, and it is also being used to enable overarching control of legacy hardware from different manufacturers.

Chapter

Final Word

A conclusion is the place where you got tired of thinking.

Albert Bloch (American Artist, 1882 – 1961)

WE wish you good luck in your endeavors. Technology is now central to most businesses strategy and operations. This means that increasingly the senior problem shapers in a business need to be technology aware – just as they need to be financially and legally aware.

IoT is one of the most exciting parts of the so called 4th Industrial Revolution. The ability to monitor and automate actions on everything from power stations to our own bodies is both fascinating and challenging. How society handles the ethical as well as business issues over the coming decades will help shape the world we live in.

We hope, for its small part, this book has provided you with a few smart questions that help you shape both your business and your personal view on where IoT can take us all.

Getting Involved

The Smart Questions community

There may be questions that we should have asked but didn't. Or specific questions which may be relevant to your situation, but not everyone in general. Let us know by sending your feedback to *feedback@smart-questions.com*. You never know, they may make it into the next edition of the book. That is a key part of the Smart Questions Philosophy.

Send us your feedback

We love feedback. We prefer great reviews, but we'll accept anything that helps take the ideas further. We welcome your comments on this book.

We'd prefer email, as it's easy to answer and saves trees. If the ideas worked for you, we'd love to hear your success stories. Maybe we could turn them into 'Talking Heads'-style video or audio interviews on our website, so others can learn from you. That's one of the reasons why we wrote this book. So, talk to us.

feedback@smart-questions.com

Got a book you need to write?

Maybe you are a domain expert with knowledge locked up inside you. You'd love to share it and there are people out there desperate for your insights. But you don't think you are an author and don't know where to start. Making it easy for you to write a book is part of the Smart Questions Philosophy.

Let us know about your book idea, and let's see if we can help you get your name in print.

potentialauthor@Smart-Questions.com

Notes pages

We hope that this book has inspired you and that you have already scribbled your thoughts all over it. However, if you have ideas that need a little more space then please use these notes pages.

Notes pages

Notes pages

www.ingramcontent.com/pod-product-compliance
Lightning Source LLC
LaVergne TN
LVHW012331060326
832902LV00011B/1839